Writing Grade 5

Best Value Books™

Table of Contents

Friendly Letters
- Robin 1
- Mallory 2
- Randy 3
- Grandfather 4
- Veterinarian 5
- Friend 6
- Choose a topic 7

Writing Paragraphs
- Making Rain 8
- New Jacket 9
- Birthdays 10
- Going to a Movie 11
- Choose a topic 12

Persuasive Paragraphs
- The Party 13
- Pancakes 14
- Karate Lessons 15
- Sleep Over 16
- Choose a topic 17

Compare/Contrast
- Window/Door 18
- Orange/Lemon 19
- Letter/Telephone 20
- Book/Movie 21
- Coat/Blanket 22
- Candle/Light Bulb 23
- Sun/Moon 24
- TV/Computer 25
- Truck/Car 26
- Choose a topic 27

Descriptive Writing
- Racecar/Rose 28
- Stream/Sandwich 29
- Bike/Apple 30
- Turtle/Pumpkin 31
- Carrot/Bunny 32
- Pizza/Ice Cream 33
- Alligator/Balloon 34
- Owl/Desert 35
- Shirts/Ocean 36
- Choose a topic 37

Constructing Stories
- Constructing Stories 1 38
- Constructing Stories 2 39
- Constructing Stories 3 40
- Constructing Stories 4 41
- Constructing Stories 5 42
- Word Box 1 43
- Word Box 2 44
- Word Box 3 45
- Word Box 4 46
- Word Box 5 47
- Word Box 6 48
- Word Box 7 49
- Story Web 1 50
- Story Web 2 51
- Story Web 3 52
- Story Web 4 53
- Story Web 5 54
- Story Web 6 55
- Choose a topic 56

Writing Stories
- Write a Story 1 57
- Write a Story 2 58
- Write a Story 3 59
- Write a Story 4 60
- Write a Story 5 61
- Write a Story 6 62
- Write a Story 7 63
- Write a Story 8 64
- Write a Story 9 65

Three Paragraph Stories
- The School Fair 66
- Camping 67
- Rub-A-Dub Dog 68
- Painting the Porch 69
- Visit to the Dentist 70
- Science Project 71
- Choose a topic 72
- Story Web 1 73
- Story Web 2 74
- Story Web 3 75
- Story Web 4 76
- Story Web 5 77
- Story Web 6 78
- Choose a topic 79

Writing Reports
- Balanced Diet 80
- Layers of the Earth 81
- Transportation 82
- Bodies in Space 83
- Storms 84
- Choose a topic 85

Point of View
- The Rescue 86
- Hang On 87
- Gotcha! 88
- Down the Drain 89
- Frog Jumping Contest 90
- At the Top 91

Character Webs
- Goldilocks 92
- Snow White 93
- Cinderella 94
- Rumplestiltskin 95
- Choose a topic 96

Book Reports
- Story elements 1 97
- Story elements 2 98
- Book review 99
- Fiction 1 100
- Fiction 2 101
- Nonfiction 102
- Biography 103
- Assignment Page 104

The student pages in this book have been specially prepared for reproduction on any standard copying machine.

Kelley Wingate products are available at fine educational supply stores throughout the U.S. and Canada.

Permission is hereby granted to the purchaser of this book to reproduce student pages for classroom use only. Reproduction for commercial resale or for an entire school or school system is strictly prohibited. No part of this book may be reproduced for storage in a retrieval system, or transmitted in any form, by any means (electronic, recording, mechanical, or otherwise) without the prior written permission of the publisher.

Writing Grade 5 CD-3720   Printed in the United States of America   ISBN 0-88724-438-6

A NOTE TO PARENTS AND TEACHERS

Children are natural storytellers. Most of them can hardly wait to recount their experiences to their teacher or friends. An important task of the parent and teacher is to turn these storytellers into story writers. Children who begin to write early become comfortable with the process. Writing becomes as natural as speaking. It is important to make writing a part of the daily schedule.

Many children find writing difficult because they do not understand how to write. They do not even know how to begin. Any writing activity must be modeled by the teacher several times before a child can grasp the concepts. To achieve the greatest affect, the activity should be conducted with a group. This allows the free exchange of ideas and prompts deeper thinking that will assist in better clarity and comprehension of the concepts. When the task is fully understood and mastered within groups, individual assignments become appropriate.

Writing is a process, and it takes time to develop ideas into a finished product. Neither the teacher nor student should expect a well designed story to emerge from an initial attempt. Teachers and students should look upon writing as a five step process. The first step is gathering ideas pertaining to the writing assignment. The second step is selecting and organizing those ideas into a rough draft. Third is the revising step to reorganize content and refine wording. The fourth step is editing (proofreading) for grammar, capitalization, and punctuation errors. Lastly, the paper is rewritten as a final copy. Remember to use these five steps to guide the writing process.

Students do willingly what they do well. Direct instruction, ample opportunities to practice skills, and exciting topics will support these storytellers in our quest to make them story writers.

About the author...

During her many years as an educator, **Rae Anne Roberson** has taught in elementary, junior and senior high, and university level settings. She is currently the Title 1 Instructional Facilitator in her school system and is helping to develop several innovative reading programs for "at risk" students in elementary schools. Rae Anne is very active as a presenter at workshops for teachers and parents. She was recently presented with the "Award for Literacy" for her school system. Certified in elementary and secondary education as well as reading specialist, Rae Anne holds an M.Ed. and is currently working toward her doctorate.

Senior Editors: Patricia Pedigo and Roger DeSanti
Production Supervisor: Homer Desrochers
Production: Arlene Evitts and Debra Ollier

Ready-To-Use Ideas and Activities

The activities in this book will help students master the basic skills necessary to become competent writers. Remember as you read through the activities listed below, and as you go through this book, that all children learn at their own rate. Although repetition is important, it is critical that we never lose sight of the fact that it is equally important to build children's self-esteem and self-confidence if we want them to become successful learners as well as good citizens.

If you are working with a child at home, try to set up a quiet comfortable environment where you will work. Make it a special time to which you each look forward. Do only a few activities at a time. Try to end each session on a positive note, and remember that fostering self-esteem and self-confidence are also critical to the learning process.

The back of this book has removable flash cards that will be great for use for basic skill and vocabulary enrichment activities. Pull the flash cards out and either cut them apart or, if you have access to a paper cutter, use that to cut the flash cards apart.

Following are checklists that students should use to help keep their sentence and paragraph writing on track.

Sentence Editing Checklist

Answer each question on this checklist either Yes or No. If your answer to any question is "No" or "I'm not sure," list that part of the report as a part that needs to be worked on.

Do most of your sentences say "who did what" and in that order?
❏ Yes ❏ No

Is every sentence complete?
❏ Yes ❏ No

Does every sentence begin with a capital letter and end with a period, question mark, or exclamation point?
❏ Yes ❏ No

Ready-To-Use Ideas and Activities

Are all your verbs in the same tense, either present or past?
❏ Yes ❏ No

Are all your sentences in the third person (unless your assignment says that you can use first or second person)?
❏ Yes ❏ No

Paragraph Editing Checklist

Answer each question on this checklist either Yes or No. If your answer to any question is "No" or "I'm not sure," list that part of your paper as a part that needs to be worked on.

Does each paragraph have a topic sentence?
❏ Yes ❏ No

Are your supporting details convincing?
❏ Yes ❏ No

Are the supporting details in logical order?
❏ Yes ❏ No

Have you tried to add special details or lively quotes?
❏ Yes ❏ No

Did you take out all dull or unnecessary information?
❏ Yes ❏ No

Have you removed sentences that don't belong with the others?
❏ Yes ❏ No

Have you double checked all punctuation?
❏ Yes ❏ No

Ready-To-Use Ideas and Activities

Use the following outline format as a guide for successful writing. Remind students that organization is one of the keys to a well written paper.

Basic Outline Format
Title

    I.   Opening
    II.   First Main Point or Idea
        A.   Supporting detail
        B.   More supporting detail
    III.   Next Main Point or Idea
        A.   Supporting detail
        B.   More supporting detail
        C.   More supporting detail
    IV.   Last Main Point or Idea
        A.   Supporting detail
        B.   More supporting detail
        C.   More supporting detail
    V.   Conclusion

Reasons For Writing

Expose your students to the many types of writing that are out in the world. Newspapers, magazines, advertisements, weather forecasts, recipes, poems, automotive manuals, short stories, novels, personal letters, and more. Once students are exposed to the many forms of writing, chances are very good that interests will peak and writing will become more enjoyable.

Creative Writing
Ask students to read an article in the newspaper. Once read, have students rewrite the article with a different ending. This exercise is extremely effective in helping students understand the importance of supporting details. Other great creative writing activities include:
- Writing letters to the school principal
- Responding to an editorial in the newspaper
- Interviewing a family member

Ready-To-Use Ideas and Activities

- Writing directions for assembling a kite
- Writing a recipe for a favorite food
- Writing a T.V. script

Correction Symbols

Symbol	Meaning	Symbol	Meaning
∧	add a word	⌒	close the space
∧ (comma)	add a comma	#	make a space
⊙	add a period	≡	capitalize
∨	add an apostrophe	/	make lower case
∨∨	add quotation marks	sp	spelling error
ℓ	remove	¶	begin a new paragraph

The Writing Process

- Pre-writing
- Rough Draft
- Revising
- Proofreading
- Publishing

Name _____   Skill: Friendly Letters

A friendly letter has 5 parts: date, greeting, body, closing, and signature.

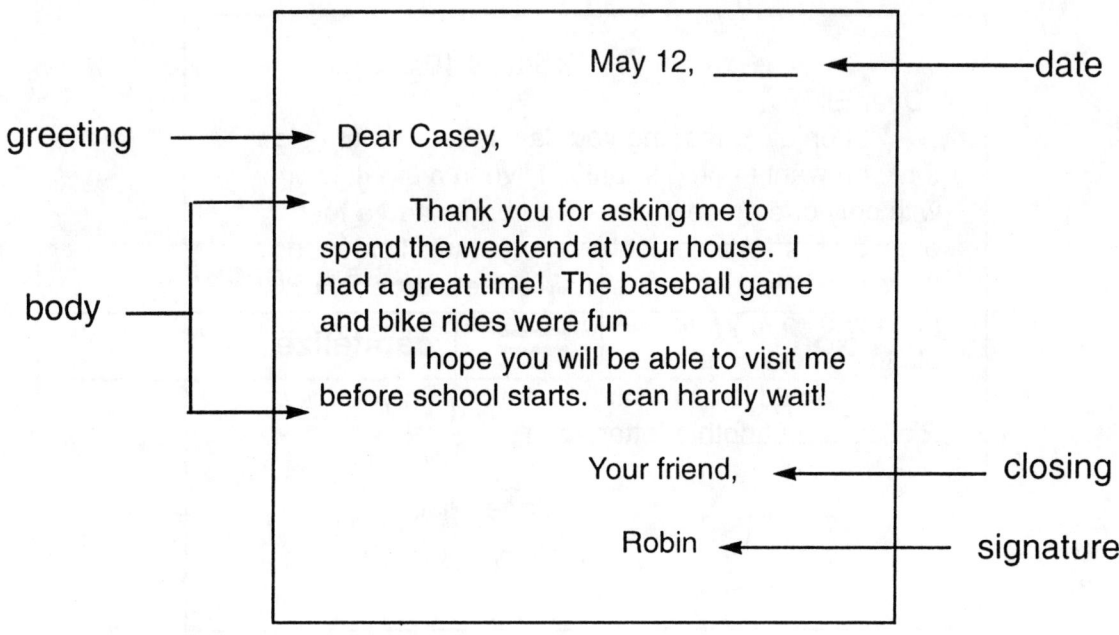

Answer Robin's letter. Talk about things you would like to do during your visit.

_____ (date)

_____ (greeting)

_____
_____
_____
_____ (body)
_____

_____ (closing)

_____ (signature)

©1996 Kelley Wingate Publications   CD-3720

Name _____   Skill: Friendly Letters

A friendly letter has 5 parts: date, greeting, body, closing, and signature.

February 10, _____

Dear Elly,

    I enjoyed reading your last letter and am glad that you want to be pen pals. I live in a small town with only one grocery store, one bank, and a few other stores. We do not have any traffic lights, but there is a stop sign at the main street corner. I can ride my bike anywhere in town because it is impossible to get lost here!

    I would like to hear about things in your city. Please write another letter soon.

Your pen pal,
Mallory

Write a letter to Mallory. Tell her about your town or city.

_____ (date)

_____ (greeting)

_____
_____
_____
_____
_____
_____ (body)

_____ (closing)

_____ (signature)

©1996 Kelley Wingate Publications

Name _____ Skill: Friendly Letters

A friendly letter has 5 parts: date, greeting, body, closing, and signature.

July 5, ____

Dear Brian,

We are starting a photography club in my school. A lot of students are interested in learning how to use their cameras to take pictures of animals and plants in our area.

We have one big problem, however. We went into the woods three times and have not seen even one animal to photograph! I know that you are great at getting pictures like this, so I thought you might have some tips for us.

Thank you,

Randy

Write a letter to Randy. Tell him what you think the problem might be.

_____ (date)

_____
(greeting)

_____
_____
_____
_____
_____ (body)

_____ (closing)

_____ (signature)

©1996 Kelley Wingate Publications   3   CD-3720

Name _____   Skill: Friendly Letters

> A friendly letter has 5 parts: date, greeting, body, closing, and signature.

1. Write a letter to your grandfather. Invite him to visit you. Include all 5 parts of a letter. Be sure to put a comma after the greeting and closing.

2. Write a letter to your cousin. Thank her for the birthday gift she sent to you. Include all 5 parts of a letter. Be sure to put a comma after the greeting and closing.

©1996 Kelley Wingate Publications   CD-3720

Name _____   Skill: Friendly Letters

> A friendly letter has 5 parts: date, greeting, body, closing, and signature.

1. You have decided that you might like to be a veterinarian one day. You have many questions about the job and have decided to write to a veterinarian and find out more. Write your questions below.

1. _____
   _____

2. _____
   _____

3. _____
   _____

4. _____
   _____

2. Use the questions to write your letter.

©1996 Kelley Wingate Publications   CD-3720

Name _____   Skill: Friendly Letters

> **A friendly letter has 5 parts: date, greeting, body, closing, and signature.**

1. You want to invite your best friend to go on a weekend camping trip with your family. There are many fun things to do, but your friend is not sure about going. Make a list of reasons why your friend should go.

1. _____
   _____

2. _____
   _____

3. _____
   _____

4. _____
   _____

2. Use the reasons you listed to write your letter.

Name _____ Skill: Friendly Letters

> **A friendly letter has 5 parts: date, greeting, body, closing, and signature.**

1. Choose a person to write to. List some of the things you want to say.

1. _____
   _____

2. _____
   _____

3. _____
   _____

4. _____
   _____

2. Use the list to write your letter.

©1996 Kelley Wingate Publications   7   CD-3720

Name _____   Skill: Writing Paragraphs

> **A paragraph contains a main idea and supporting details.**

Every paragraph has one main idea. The main idea is called the **topic sentence**. It is usually the first sentence in the paragraph. The other sentences are **details** that tell more about the main idea. The last sentence retells the main idea.

1. Read over the information given below.

Title of paragraph:	Making Rain

Main Idea:	We made rain in my science class today.

Details:
1. First we froze a metal pie pan of water.
2. Next we heated another pan of water until it steamed.
3. We held the frozen water pie pan over the steam.
4. When the steam touched it, water formed on the frozen pie pan and fell like rain.

Retell Main Idea: Making rain was easy and fun.

2. Use the above information to write a paragraph. Write the main idea, add the details, then retell the main idea. Indent the first sentence. Use capitals and periods. Remember to give the paragraph a title.

_____

_____

_____
_____
_____
_____
_____
_____
_____
_____

©1996 Kelley Wingate Publications   CD-3720

Name _____   Skill: Writing Paragraphs

> A paragraph contains a main idea and supporting details.

Every paragraph has one main idea. The main idea is called the **topic sentence**. It is usually the first sentence in the paragraph. The other sentences are **details** that tell more about the main idea. The last sentence retells the main idea.

1. Read over the information given below.

Title of paragraph: Shopping for a New Jacket

Main Idea: Mom and I went to the mall to buy a new jacket.

Details:
    1. First we went to my favorite store.
    2. I found six jackets that I really liked.
    3. I tried on each jacket and looked in the mirror.
    4. Mom and I agreed on which one we liked best.
    5. We bought the jacket.

Retell Main Idea: My mom and I picked out a new a jacket for me.

2. Use these sentences to write a paragraph. Write the main idea, add the details, then retell the main idea. Indent the first sentence. Use capitals and periods. Remember to give the paragraph a title.

©1996 Kelley Wingate Publications   CD-3720

Name _____   Skill: Writing Paragraphs

> **A paragraph contains a main idea and supporting details.**

Every paragraph has one main idea. The main idea is called the **topic sentence**. It is usually the first sentence in the paragraph. The other sentences are **details** that tell more about the main idea. The last sentence retells the main idea.

Look at the title and main idea of the paragraph. Write your own details.

Title of paragraph: Birthdays Are Special

Main Idea: At my house, birthdays are special.

Details:
1. _____
2. _____
3. _____
4. _____

Retell Main Idea: I can hardly wait for my birthday!

_____

2. Use these sentences to write a paragraph. Write the main idea, add the details, then retell the main idea. Indent the first sentence. Use capitals and periods. Remember to give the paragraph a title.

_____

_____
_____
_____
_____
_____
_____
_____
_____

Name _____   Skill: Writing Paragraphs

> **A paragraph contains a main idea and supporting details.**

Every paragraph has one main idea. The main idea is called the **topic sentence**. It is usually the first sentence in the paragraph. The other sentences are **details** that tell more about the main idea. The last sentence retells the main idea.

1. Look at the title and main idea of the paragraph. Write your own details.

Title of paragraph: <u>Going to a Movie</u>

Main Idea: I love to go to the movie theater on Saturday.

Details:
1. _____
2. _____
3. _____
4. _____

Retell Main Idea: Going to a movie makes Saturday a special day.

---

2. Use these sentences to write a paragraph. Write the main idea, add the details, then retell the main idea. Indent the first sentence. Use capitals and periods. Remember to give the paragraph a title.

_____

_____
_____
_____
_____
_____
_____
_____
_____

©1996 Kelley Wingate Publications

Name _____   Skill: Writing Paragraphs

> **A paragraph contains a main idea and supporting details.**

Every paragraph has one main idea. The main idea is called the **topic sentence**. It is usually the first sentence in the paragraph. The other sentences are **details** that tell more about the main idea. The last sentence retells the main idea.

1. **Choose an idea for your paragraph. Write the title, main idea, and details. Retell the main idea at the end.**

Title of paragraph: _____

Main Idea: _____

Details: 1. _____
                    2. _____
                    3. _____
                    4. _____

Retell Main Idea: _____

2. **Use the above information to write a paragraph. Write the main idea, add the details, then retell the main idea. Indent the first sentence. Use capitals and periods. Remember to give the paragraph a title.**

_____

_____

_____

_____

_____

_____

_____

_____

©1996 Kelley Wingate Publications

Name _____   Skill: Persuasive Paragraphs

A paragraph contains a main idea and supporting details.

Some paragraphs are written to persuade, or change the way people think. These paragraphs have a main idea and supporting details.

---

1. You must convince your parents to let you have a party. Ask them, give your reasons, then ask again.

Title :   The Party

Question: May I have a party this Saturday afternoon?

Reasons: 1. I will invite only people you know.
                      2. I will clean the house before and after the party.
                      3. I will fix all of the snacks myself.
                      4. We will follow all of the house rules.

Ask again: Is it all right with you if I have a party this Saturday?

---

2. Use the above information to write a paragraph. Write the main idea, add the details, then retell the main idea. Indent the first sentence. Use capitals and periods. Remember to give the paragraph a title.

_____

_____
_____
_____
_____
_____
_____
_____
_____

©1996 Kelley Wingate Publications

Name _____   Skill: Persuasive Paragraphs

> **A paragraph contains a main idea and supporting details.**

Some paragraphs are written to persuade, or change the way people think. These paragraphs have a main idea and supporting details.

---

1. You must convince your mom to make pancakes for breakfast. Ask her, give your reasons, then ask again.

Title :   <u>Pancakes for Breakfast</u>

Question: Will you make pancakes for breakfast, Mom?

Reasons: 1. I will help you cook them.
2. I will wash the dishes after breakfast.
3. We haven't had them in a long time.
4. You make the best pancakes I've ever eaten.

Ask again: May we have pancakes for breakfast this morning?

---

2. Use the above information to write a paragraph. Write the main idea, add the details, then retell the main idea. Indent the first sentence. Use capitals and periods. Remember to give the paragraph a title.

_____

_____

_____

_____

_____

_____

_____

_____

_____

Name _____   Skill: Persuasive Paragraphs

A paragraph contains a main idea and supporting details.

Some paragraphs are written to persuade, or change the way people think. These paragraphs have a main idea and supporting details.

1. You must convince your dad to let you take karate lessons. Ask him, give your reasons, then ask again.

Title :   <u>Karate Lessons</u>

Question: May I _____

Reasons: 1. _____
                 2. _____
                 3. _____
                 4. _____

Ask again: _____

2. Use the above information to write a paragraph. Write the main idea, add the details, then retell the main idea. Indent the first sentence. Use capitals and periods. Remember to give the paragraph a title.

_____

_____
_____
_____
_____
_____
_____
_____
_____
_____

©1996 Kelley Wingate Publications

Name _____   Skill: Persuasive Paragraphs

> **A paragraph contains a main idea and supporting details.**

Some paragraphs are written to persuade, or change the way people think. These paragraphs have a main idea and supporting details.

---

1. You must convince your mom to let you stay at a friend's house tonight. Ask her, give your reasons, then ask again.

Title : _____

Question: May I _____

Reasons: 1. _____
            2. _____
            3. _____
            4. _____

Ask again: _____

2. Use the above information to write a paragraph. Write the main idea, add the details, then retell the main idea. Indent the first sentence. Use capitals and periods. Remember to give the paragraph a title.

_____

_____
_____
_____
_____
_____
_____
_____
_____
_____

Name _____   Skill: Persuasive Paragraphs

> **A paragraph contains a main idea and supporting details.**

Some paragraphs are written to persuade, or change the way people think. These paragraphs have a main idea and supporting details.

1. Choose a topic and ask a question. Give your reasons, then ask again.

Topic: _____

Question: May I _____

Reasons: 1. _____
             2. _____
             3. _____
             4. _____

Ask again: _____

2. Use these sentences to write a paragraph. Write the main idea, add the details, then retell the main idea. Indent the first sentence. Use capitals and periods. Remember to give the paragraph a title.

_____

_____
_____
_____
_____
_____
_____
_____
_____
_____

Name _____   Skill: Compare and Contrast

Some things can be both alike and different.

1. Complete the circles by comparing and contrasting a window and a door.

window **contrast**	**compare**	door **contrast**
1. made of glass	1. opens	1. made of wood
2. smooth	2. in a wall	2. has a knob or handle
3. breaks easily	3. part of a building	3. swings on hinges

2. Write 2 paragraphs below. In the first paragraph tell how windows and doors are alike. Tell how each is different in the second paragraph. Indent the first sentence. Title your story.

_____

_____
_____
_____
_____
_____
_____
_____
_____
_____
_____
_____

©1996 Kelley Wingate Publications

Name _____   Skill: Compare and Contrast

Some things can be both alike and different.

1. Complete the circles by comparing and contrasting an orange and a lemon.

orange	lemon
contrast	**compare**	**contrast**
1. orange	1. juicy	1. yellow
2. round	2. has a peel	2. oval
3. sweet	3. has seeds	3. sour

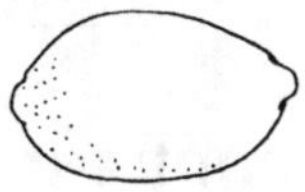

1. Write 2 paragraphs below. In the first paragraph tell how oranges and lemons are alike. Tell how each is different in the second paragraph. Indent the first sentence. Title your story.

_____

_____
_____
_____
_____
_____
_____
_____
_____
_____

©1996 Kelley Wingate Publications   CD-3720

Name _____   Skill: Compare and Contrast

Some things can be both alike and different.

1. Complete the circles by comparing and contrasting a letter and a telephone.

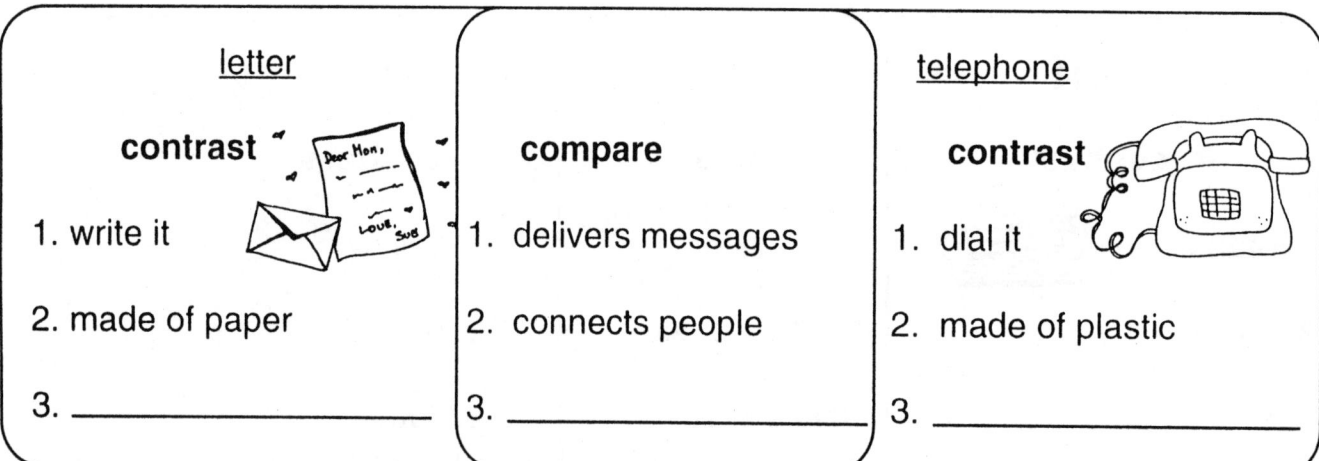

letter		telephone
contrast	**compare**	**contrast**
1. write it	1. delivers messages	1. dial it
2. made of paper	2. connects people	2. made of plastic
3. _____	3. _____	3. _____

2. Write 2 paragraphs below. In the first paragraph tell how a letter and a telephone are alike. Tell how each is different in the second paragraph. Indent the first sentence. Title your story.

_____

_____
_____
_____
_____
_____
_____
_____
_____
_____
_____
_____

Name _____   Skill: Compare and Contrast

Some things can be both alike and different.

1. Complete the circles by comparing and contrasting a book and a movie.

book		movie
contrast	**compare**	**contrast**
1. read it	1. tell a story	1. watch it
2. on paper	2. entertains	2. on a screen
3. _____	3. _____	3. _____

2. Write 2 paragraphs below. In the first paragraph tell how a book and a movie are alike. Tell how each is different in the second paragraph. Indent the first sentence. Title your story.

_____

_____
_____
_____
_____
_____
_____
_____
_____
_____
_____

©1996 Kelley Wingate Publications   CD-3720

Name _____   Skill: Compare and Contrast

> Some things can be both alike and different.

1. Complete the circles by comparing and contrasting a coat and a blanket.

coat

contrast
1. wear it
2. _____
3. _____

compare
1. keeps you warm
2. _____
3. _____

blanket

contrast
1. cover up with it
2. _____
3. _____

2. Write 2 paragraphs below. In the first paragraph tell how a coat and a blanket are alike. Tell how each is different in the second paragraph. Indent the first sentence. Title your story.

_____

_____
_____
_____
_____
_____
_____
_____
_____
_____
_____

Name _____   Skill: Compare and Contrast

Some things can be both alike and different.

1. **Complete the circles by comparing and contrasting a candle and a light bulb.**

candle 	compare	light bulb 
contrast		**contrast**
1. made of wax	1. gives off light	1. made of glass
2. _____	2. _____	2. _____
3. _____	3. _____	3. _____

2. **Write 2 paragraphs below. In the first paragraph tell how a candle and a light bulb are alike. Tell how each is different in the second paragraph. Indent the first sentence. Title your story.**

_____

_____
_____
_____
_____
_____
_____
_____
_____
_____
_____
_____

Name _____   Skill: Compare and Contrast

Some things can be both alike and different.

1. Complete the circles by comparing and contrasting the sun and the moon.

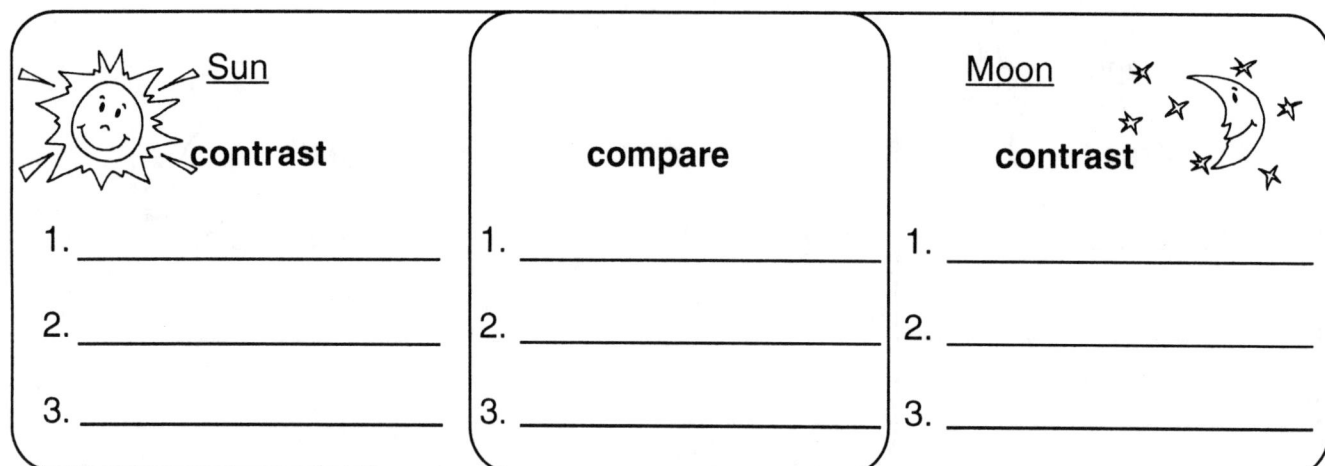

2. Write 2 paragraphs below. In the first paragraph tell how the sun and the moon are alike. Tell how each is different in the second paragraph. Indent the first sentence. Title your story.

_____

_____
_____
_____
_____
_____
_____
_____
_____
_____
_____
_____
_____

Name _____   Skill: Compare and Contrast

Some things can be both alike and different.

1. Complete the circles by comparing and contrasting a computer and a television.

television	compare	computer
contrast	1. _____	contrast
1. _____	2. _____	1. _____
2. _____	3. _____	2. _____
3. _____		3. _____

2. Write 2 paragraphs below. In the first paragraph tell how a television and a computer are alike. Tell how each is different in the second paragraph. Indent the first sentence. Title your story.

_____

_____
_____
_____
_____
_____
_____
_____
_____
_____
_____

Name _____   Skill: Compare and Contrast

| **Some things can be both alike and different.** |

1. Complete the circles by comparing and contrasting an truck and a car.

truck	compare	car
contrast	**compare**	**contrast**
1. _____	1. _____	1. _____
2. _____	2. _____	2. _____
3. _____	3. _____	3. _____

2. Write 2 paragraphs below. In the first paragraph tell how an truck and a car are alike. Tell how each is different in the second paragraph. Indent the first sentence. Title your story.

_____

_____
_____
_____
_____
_____
_____
_____
_____
_____
_____
_____

Name _____   Skill: Compare and Contrast

Some things can be both alike and different.

1. Choose your own topic to compare and contrast.

_____	_____	_____
contrast	compare	contrast
1. _____	1. _____	1. _____
2. _____	2. _____	2. _____
3. _____	3. _____	3. _____

2. Write 2 paragraphs below. In the first paragraph tell how these two things are alike. Tell how each is different in the second paragraph. Indent the first sentence. Title your story.

_____

_____
_____
_____
_____
_____
_____
_____
_____
_____

©1996 Kelley Wingate Publications   CD-3720

Name _____ Skill: Descriptive Writing

Adjectives are words that describe which, how many, what color, or what an object looks or feels like.

Adjectives make stories more colorful and interesting. They help you "see" a story in your imagination.

Write a paragraph about each picture using the adjectives listed beside it. Write a title for your paragraph.

1. speedy 2. hot
3. roaring 4. screeching
5. shiny

_____

_____
_____
_____
_____
_____
_____

1. sweet 2. soft
3. picky 4. sharp
5. thorny

_____

_____
_____
_____
_____
_____

©1996 Kelley Wingate Publications

Name _____   Skill: Descriptive Writing

> **Adjectives are words that describe which, how many, what color, or what an object looks or feels like.**

Adjectives make stories more colorful and interesting. They help you "see" a story in your imagination.

Write a paragraph about each picture using the adjectives listed beside it. Write a title for your paragraph.

1. splashing 2. rocky
3. icy cold 4. clear
5. gurgling

_____

_____
_____
_____
_____
_____
_____

1. juicy 2. greasy
3. tasty 4. mouth watering
5. melted cheese

_____

_____
_____
_____
_____
_____
_____

Name _____   Skill: Descriptive Writing

> **Adjectives are words that describe which, how many, what color, or what an object looks or feels like.**

Adjectives make stories more colorful and interesting. They help you "see" a story in your imagination.

Four adjectives are listed for each picture below. Add an adjective of your own. Write a paragraph about each picture using the adjectives.

1. fun   2. sparkling
3. new   4. fast
5. _____

_____
_____
_____
_____
_____
_____

1. red   2. round
3. juicy   4. healthy
5. _____

_____
_____
_____
_____
_____

©1996 Kelley Wingate Publications   CD-3720

Name _____   Skill: Descriptive Writing

> **Adjectives are words that describe which, how many, what color, or what an object looks or feels like.**

Adjectives make stories more colorful and interesting. They help you "see" a story in your imagination.

Four adjectives are listed for each picture below. Add an adjective of your own. Write a paragraph about each picture using the adjectives.

1. green
2. friendly
3. slow
4. hard shelled
5. _____

_____
_____
_____
_____
_____
_____

1. round
2. orange
3. bumpy
4. scary
5. _____

_____
_____
_____
_____
_____
_____

©1996 Kelley Wingate Publications   CD-3720

Name _____   Skill: Descriptive Writing

Adjectives are words that describe which, how many, what color, or what an object looks or feels like.

Adjectives make stories more colorful and interesting. They help you "see" a story in your imagination.

Three adjectives are listed for each picture below. Add two adjectives of your own. Write a paragraph about each picture using the adjectives.

1. orange   2. delicious

3. long   4. _____

               5. _____

_____

_____
_____
_____
_____
_____

1. furry   2. long-eared

3. cute   4. _____

      5. _____

_____
_____
_____
_____
_____

©1996 Kelley Wingate Publications   CD-3720

Name _____   Skill: Descriptive Writing

> **Adjectives are words that describe which, how many, what color, or what an object looks or feels like.**

Adjectives make stories more colorful and interesting. They help you "see" a story in your imagination.

Three adjectives are listed for each picture below. Add two adjectives of your own. Write a paragraph about each picture using the adjectives.

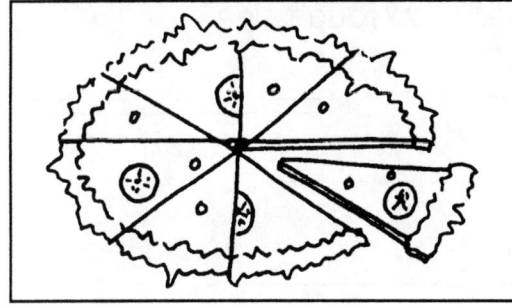

1. hot   2. flavorful
3. round   4. _____
         5. _____

_____
_____
_____
_____
_____
_____
_____

1. cold   2. wet
3. sticky   4. _____
         5. _____

_____
_____
_____
_____
_____
_____

Name _____   Skill: Descriptive Writing

> **Adjectives are words that describe which, how many, what color, or what an object looks or feels like.**

Adjectives make stories more colorful and interesting. They help you "see" a story in your imagination.

Two adjectives are listed for each picture below. Add three adjectives of your own. Write a paragraph about each picture using the adjectives.

1. green   2. rough skin
3. _____   4. _____
5. _____

_____
_____
_____
_____
_____
_____
_____

1. fragile   2. light
3. _____   4. _____
5. _____

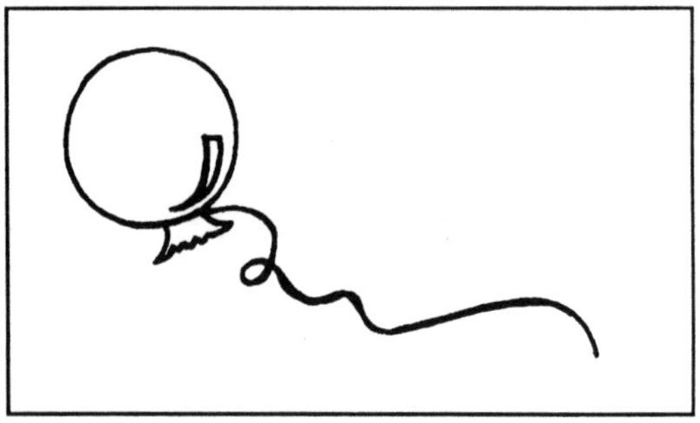

_____
_____
_____
_____
_____
_____

Name _____   Skill: Descriptive Writing

Adjectives are words that describe which, how many, what color, or what an object looks or feels like.

Adjectives make stories more colorful and interesting. They help you "see" a story in your imagination.

Two adjectives are listed for each picture below. Add three adjectives of your own. Write a paragraph about each picture using the adjectives.

1. feathered   2. wise

3. _____   4. _____

5. _____

_____
_____
_____
_____
_____
_____
_____

1. sandy   2. hot

3. _____   4. _____

5. _____

_____
_____
_____
_____
_____
_____

©1996 Kelley Wingate Publications   CD-3720

Name _____   Skill: Descriptive Writing

> **Adjectives are words that describe which, how many, what color, or what an object looks or feels like.**

Adjectives make stories more colorful and interesting. They help you "see" a story in your imagination.

For each picture, write five adjectives to describe it. Write a paragraph about each picture using the adjectives. Give each paragraph a title.

1. _____ 2. _____
3. _____ 4. _____
5. _____

_____

_____
_____
_____
_____
_____
_____
_____

1. _____ 2. _____
3. _____ 4. _____
5. _____

_____

_____
_____
_____
_____
_____
_____
_____

©1996 Kelley Wingate Publications   CD-3720

Name _____ Skill: Descriptive Writing

Adjectives are words that describe which, how many, what color, or what an object looks or feels like.

Adjectives make stories more colorful and interesting. They help you "see" a story in your imagination.

Draw or paste a picture in each box then write five adjectives that describe each picture. Write a paragraph about each picture using the adjectives.

1. _____ 2. _____
3. _____ 4. _____
5. _____

_____

_____
_____
_____
_____
_____
_____

1. _____ 2. _____
3. _____ 4. _____
5. _____

_____

_____
_____
_____
_____
_____

©1996 Kelley Wingate Publications 37 CD-3720

Name _____   Skill: Constructing Stories

| **Stories have a beginning, a middle, and an end** |

1. Make up your own story by answering the questions about the picture. Use adjectives for description. Write in complete sentences.

1. Who or what is this story about? _____
_____
_____

2. Where does this story take place? _____
_____
_____

3. How does this story begin? _____
_____
_____

4. What will happen next? _____
_____

5. How will the story end? _____
_____

2. Write a story using your sentences. Be sure to use capitals and periods. Remember to indent the first line. Title your story.

_____

_____
_____
_____
_____
_____
_____
_____

©1996 Kelley Wingate Publications   CD-3720

Name _____   Skill: Constructing Stories

| Stories have a beginning, a middle, and an end |

1. Make up your own story by answering the questions about the picture. Use adjectives for description. Write in complete sentences.

1. Who or what is this story about? _____
   _____
   _____

2. Where does this story take place? _____
   _____
   _____

3. How does this story begin? _____
   _____
   _____

4. What will happen next? _____
   _____

5. How will the story end? _____
   _____

2. Write a story using your sentences. Be sure to use capitals and periods. Remember to indent the first line. Title your story.

_____

_____
_____
_____
_____
_____
_____
_____
_____

Name _____   Skill: Constructing Stories

| Stories have a beginning, a middle, and an end |

1. Make up your own story by answering the questions about the picture. Use adjectives for description. Write in complete sentences.

1. Who or what is this story about? _____
   _____
   _____

2. Where does this story take place? _____
   _____
   _____

3. How does this story begin? _____
   _____
   _____

4. What will happen next? _____
   _____

5. How will the story end? _____
   _____

2. Write a story using your sentences. Be sure to use capitals and periods. Remember to indent the first line. Title your story.

_____

_____
_____
_____
_____
_____
_____
_____

©1996 Kelley Wingate Publications   CD-3720

Name _____   Skill: Constructing Stories

| Stories have a beginning, a middle, and an end |

1. Make up your own story by answering the questions about the picture. Use adjectives for description. Write complete sentences.

1. Who or what is this story about? _____
   _____
   _____

2. Where does this story take place? _____
   _____
   _____

3. How does this story begin? _____
   _____
   _____

4. What will happen next? _____
   _____

5. How will the story end? _____
   _____

2. Write a story using your sentences. Be sure to use capitals and periods. Remember to indent the first line. Title your story.

_____

_____
_____
_____
_____
_____
_____
_____
_____

©1996 Kelley Wingate Publications   CD-3720

Name _____   Skill: Constructing Stories

> **Stories have a beginning, a middle, and an end**

1. Make up your own story by answering the questions about the picture. Use adjectives for description. Write complete sentences.

1. Who or what is this story about? _____
   _____
   _____

2. Where does this story take place? _____
   _____
   _____

3. How does this story begin? _____
   _____
   _____

4. What will happen next? _____
   _____

5. How will the story end? _____
   _____

2. Write a story using your sentences. Be sure to use capitals and periods. Remember to indent the first line. Title your story.

_____

_____
_____
_____
_____
_____
_____
_____

©1996 Kelley Wingate Publications   CD-3720

Name _____   Skill: Word Box Stories

| Stories have a beginning, a middle, and an end |

Add 3 more words about this picture to the word box. Use the words to write a story. Be sure to use adjectives, capitals, and periods. Title your story.

THINGS TO THINK ABOUT
Who is this story about? Where does this story take place? How does this story begin? What happens next? How will you make this story end?

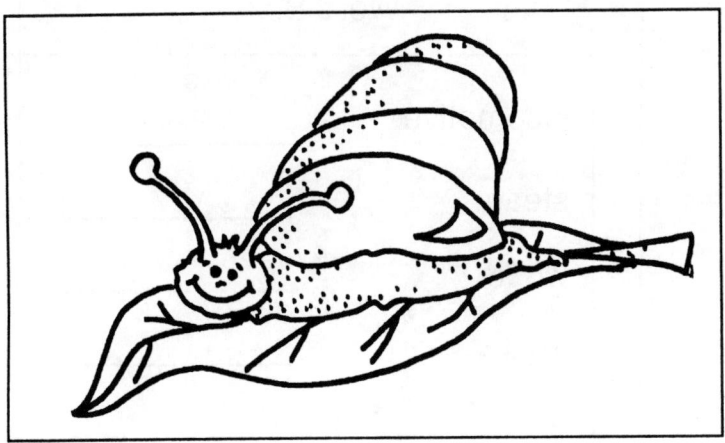

Word Box

antlers	leaves
shell	_____
swirling	_____
slow	_____

_____

_____
_____
_____
_____
_____
_____
_____
_____

©1996 Kelley Wingate Publications   CD-3720

Name _____   Skill: Word Box Stories

Stories have a beginning, a middle, and an end

Add 4 more words about this picture to the word box. Use the words to write a story. Be sure to use adjectives, capitals, and periods. Title your story.

THINGS TO THINK ABOUT
Who is this story about? Where does this story take place? How does this story begin? What happens next? How will you make this story end?

Word Box

locomotive	_____
steam	_____
wood	_____
tracks	_____

©1996 Kelley Wingate Publications CD-3720

Name _____   Skill: Word Box Stories

Stories have a beginning, a middle, and an end

Add 5 more words about this picture to the word box. Use the words to write a story. Be sure to use adjectives, capitals, and periods. Title your story.

THINGS TO THINK ABOUT
Who is this story about? Where does this story take place? How does this story begin? What happens next? How will you make this story end?

Word Box

race _____
fast _____
tie _____
_____ _____

©1996 Kelley Wingate Publications   CD-3720

Name _____ Skill: Word Box Stories

Stories have a beginning, a middle, and an end

Add 6 more words about this picture to the word box. Use the words to write a story. Be sure to use adjectives, capitals, and periods. Title your story.

THINGS TO THINK ABOUT
Who is this story about? Where does this story take place? How does this story begin? What happens next? How will you make this story end?

Word Box

raincoat _____

puddles _____

_____ _____

_____ _____

©1996 Kelley Wingate Publications   CD-3720

Name _____ Skill: Word Box Stories

| Stories have a beginning, a middle, and an end |

Add 6 more words about this picture to the word box. Use the words to write a story. Be sure to use adjectives, capitals, and periods. Title your story.

THINGS TO THINK ABOUT
Who is this story about? Where does this story take place? How does this story begin? What happens next? How will you make this story end?

Word Box

moat _____

knights _____

_____ _____

_____ _____

_____

_____
_____
_____
_____
_____
_____
_____
_____

©1996 Kelley Wingate Publications   47   CD-3720

Name _____   Skill: Word Box Stories

Stories have a beginning, a middle, and an end

Add 6 more words about this picture to the word box. Use the words to write a story. Be sure to use adjectives, capitals, and periods. Title your story.

THINGS TO THINK ABOUT
Who is this story about? Where does this story take place? How does this story begin? What happens next? How will you make this story end?

Word Box

farm   _____

morning _____

_____ _____

_____ _____

©1996 Kelley Wingate Publications   CD-3720

Name _____   Skill: Word Box Stories

Stories have a beginning, a middle, and an end

Add 8 words about this picture to the word box. Use the words to write a story. Be sure to use adjectives, capitals, and periods. Title your story.

THINGS TO THINK ABOUT
Who is this story about? Where does this story take place? How does this story begin? What happens next? How will you make this story end?

Word Box

©1996 Kelley Wingate Publications — CD-3720

Name _____   Skill: Story Web

Stories have a beginning, a middle, and an end

Use the words in the web to write a story about the picture. Be sure to use capitals and periods. Title your story.

THINGS TO THINK ABOUT
Who is this story about? Where does this story take place? How does this story begin? What happens next? How will you make this story end?

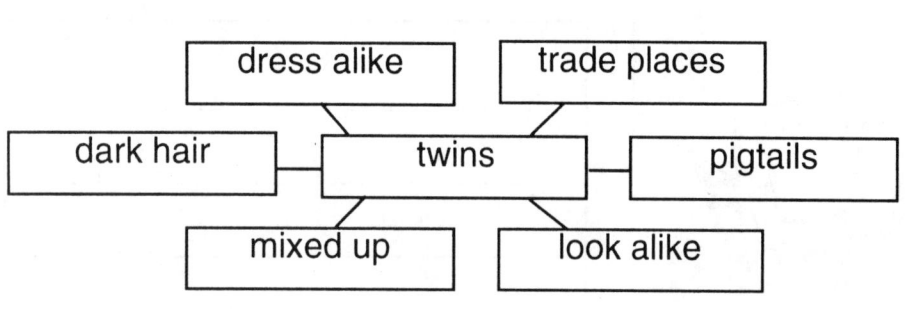

©1996 Kelley Wingate Publications   50   CD-3720

Name _____   Skill: Story Web

Stories have a beginning, a middle, and an end

Finish the story web. Use the words in the web to write a story about the picture. Be sure to use capitals and periods. Title your story.

THINGS TO THINK ABOUT
Who is this story about? Where does this story take place? How does this story begin? What happens next? How will you make this story end?

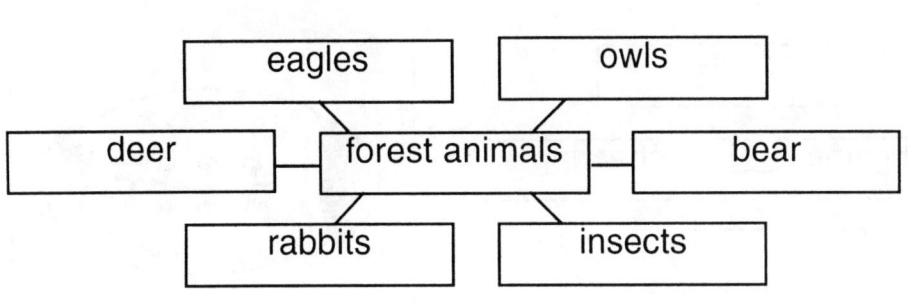

Name _____   Skill: Story Web

| Stories have a beginning, a middle, and an end |

Finish the story web. Use the words in the web to write a story about the picture. Be sure to use capitals and periods. Title your story.

THINGS TO THINK ABOUT
Who is this story about? Where does this story take place? How does this story begin? What happens next? How will you make this story end?

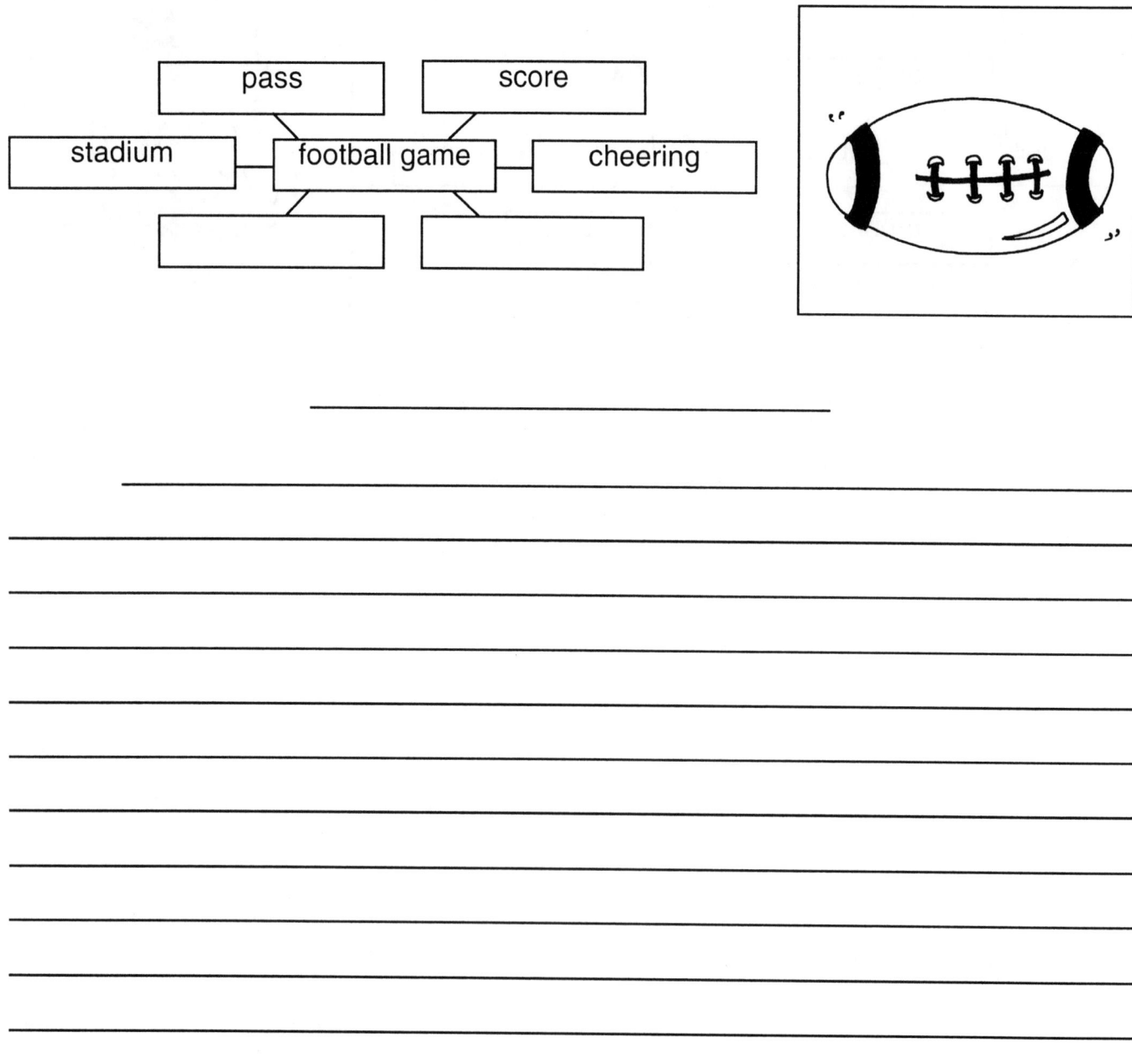

©1996 Kelley Wingate Publications   52   CD-3720

Name _____   Skill: Story Web

Stories have a beginning, a middle, and an end

Finish the story web. Use the words in the web to write a story about the picture. Be sure to use capitals and periods. Title your story.

THINGS TO THINK ABOUT
Who is this story about? Where does this story take place? How does this story begin? What happens next? How will you make this story end?

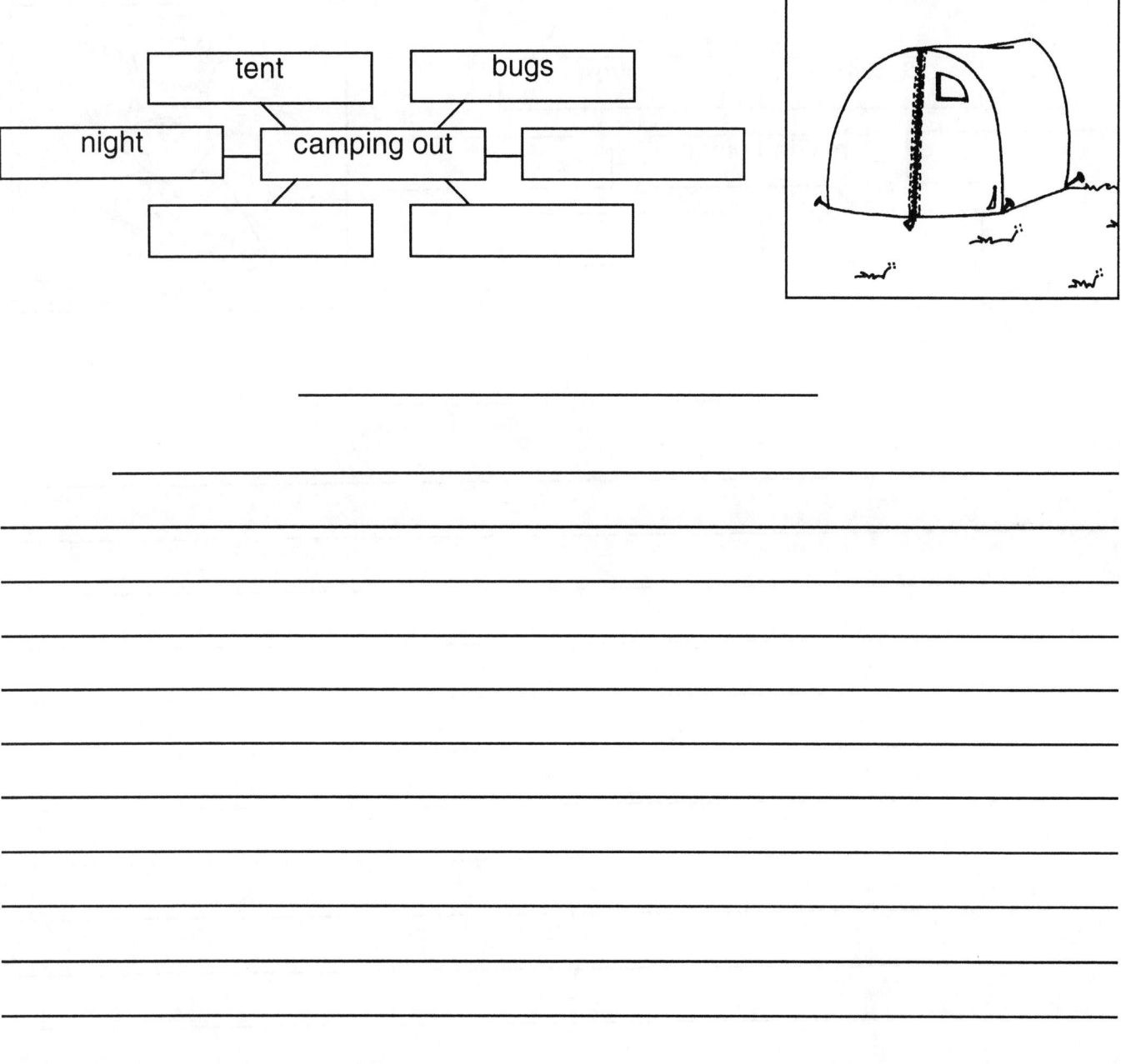

Name _____   Skill: Story Web

| Stories have a beginning, a middle, and an end |

Finish the story web. Use the words in the web to write a story about the picture. Be sure to use capitals and periods. Title your story.

THINGS TO THINK ABOUT
Who is this story about? Where does this story take place? How does this story begin? What happens next? How will you make this story end?

_____

_____
_____
_____
_____
_____
_____
_____
_____
_____
_____

©1996 Kelley Wingate Publications

Name _____ Skill: Story Web

| Stories have a beginning, a middle, and an end |

Finish the story web. Use the words in the web to write a story about the picture. Be sure to use capitals and periods. Title your story.

THINGS TO THINK ABOUT
Who is this story about? Where does this story take place? How does this story begin? What happens next? How will you make this story end?

©1996 Kelley Wingate Publications   CD-3720

Name _____   Skill: Story Web

Stories have a beginning, a middle, and an end

Choose a topic and finish the story web. Use the words in the web to write a story. Be sure to use capitals and periods. Title your story.

THINGS TO THINK ABOUT
Who is this story about? Where does this story take place? How does this story begin? What happens next? How will you make this story end?

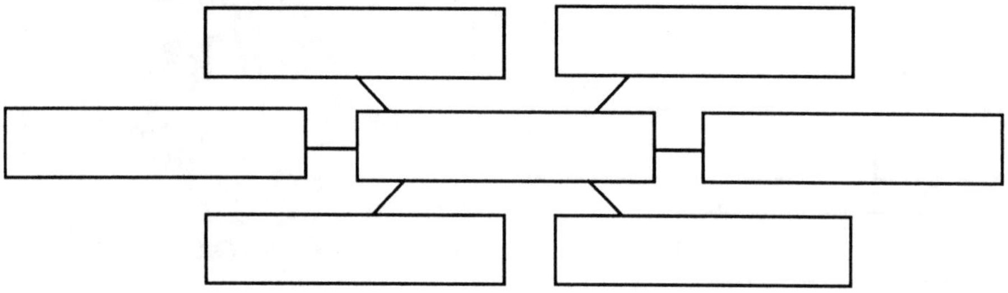

_____

_____
_____
_____
_____
_____
_____
_____
_____
_____
_____

Name _____

Skill: Writing Stories

THINGS TO THINK ABOUT FOR EVERY STORY:

★ Sentences begin with capitals and end with periods, question marks, or exclamation marks.
★ A paragraph contains a main idea and supporting details.
★ The first sentence of a paragraph should be indented.
★ Adjectives make stories more colorful and interesting.
★ A story tells who did what, when and where it was done, how it happened, and why it happened.
★ Stories have a beginning, a middle, and an end.

Write a story about the picture below. Be sure to follow all the hints in the "Things to Think About" box. Give your story a title.

©1996 Kelley Wingate Publications   CD-3720

Name _____   Skill: Writing Stories

> **THINGS TO THINK ABOUT FOR EVERY STORY:**
>
> ★ Sentences begin with capitals and end with periods, question marks, or exclamation marks.
> ★ A paragraph contains a main idea and supporting details.
> ★ The first sentence of a paragraph should be indented.
> ★ Adjectives make stories more colorful and interesting.
> ★ A story tells who did what, when and where it was done, how it happened, and why it happened.
> ★ Stories have a beginning, a middle, and an end.

Write a story about the picture below. Be sure to follow all the hints in the "Things to Think About" box. Give your story a title.

Name _____ Skill: Writing Stories

THINGS TO THINK ABOUT FOR EVERY STORY:

★ Sentences begin with capitals and end with periods, question marks, or exclamation marks.
★ A paragraph contains a main idea and supporting details.
★ The first sentence of a paragraph should be indented.
★ Adjectives make stories more colorful and interesting.
★ A story tells who did what, when and where it was done, how it happened, and why it happened.
★ Stories have a beginning, a middle, and an end.

Write a story about the picture below. Be sure to follow all the hints in the "Things to Think About" box. Give your story a title.

©1996 Kelley Wingate Publications   59   CD-3720

Name _____ Skill: Writing Stories

THINGS TO THINK ABOUT FOR EVERY STORY:

★ Sentences begin with capitals and end with periods, question marks, or exclamation marks.
★ A paragraph contains a main idea and supporting details.
★ The first sentence of a paragraph should be indented.
★ Adjectives make stories more colorful and interesting.
★ A story tells who did what, when and where it was done, how it happened, and why it happened.
★ Stories have a beginning, a middle, and an end.

Write a story about the picture below. Be sure to follow all the hints in the "Things to Think About" box. Give your story a title.

©1996 Kelley Wingate Publications   CD-3720

Name _____

Skill: Writing Stories

THINGS TO THINK ABOUT FOR EVERY STORY:

★ Sentences begin with capitals and end with periods, question marks, or exclamation marks.
★ A paragraph contains a main idea and supporting details.
★ The first sentence of a paragraph should be indented.
★ Adjectives make stories more colorful and interesting.
★ A story tells who did what, when and where it was done, how it happened, and why it happened.
★ Stories have a beginning, a middle, and an end.

Write a story about the picture below. Be sure to follow all the hints in the "Things to Think About" box. Give your story a title.

©1996 Kelley Wingate Publications   CD-3720

Name _____ Skill: Writing Stories

> **THINGS TO THINK ABOUT FOR EVERY STORY:**
>
> ★ Sentences begin with capitals and end with periods, question marks, or exclamation marks.
> ★ A paragraph contains a main idea and supporting details.
> ★ The first sentence of a paragraph should be indented.
> ★ Adjectives make stories more colorful and interesting.
> ★ A story tells who did what, when and where it was done, how it happened, and why it happened.
> ★ Stories have a beginning, a middle, and an end.

Write a story about the picture below. Be sure to follow all the hints in the "Things to Think About" box. Give your story a title.

Name _____   Skill: Writing Stories

THINGS TO THINK ABOUT FOR EVERY STORY:

★ Sentences begin with capitals and end with periods, question marks, or exclamation marks.
★ A paragraph contains a main idea and supporting details.
★ The first sentence of a paragraph should be indented.
★ Adjectives make stories more colorful and interesting.
★ A story tells who did what, when and where it was done, how it happened, and why it happened.
★ Stories have a beginning, a middle, and an end.

Write a story about the picture below. Be sure to follow all the hints in the "Things to Think About" box. Give your story a title.

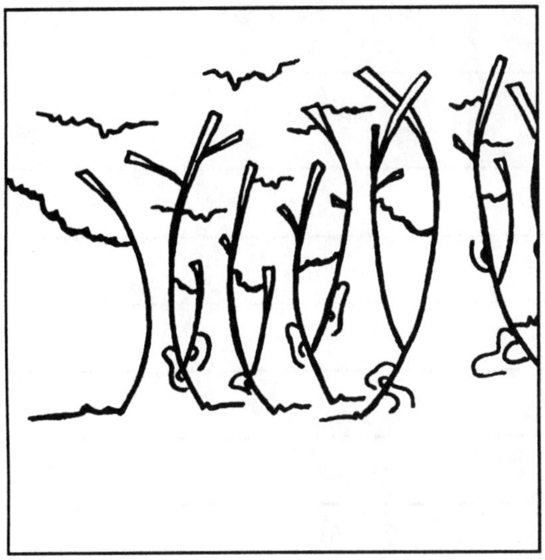

Name _____ Skill: Writing Stories

> **THINGS TO THINK ABOUT FOR EVERY STORY:**
>
> ★ Sentences begin with capitals and end with periods, question marks, or exclamation marks.
> ★ A paragraph contains a main idea and supporting details.
> ★ The first sentence of a paragraph should be indented.
> ★ Adjectives make stories more colorful and interesting.
> ★ A story tells who did what, when and where it was done, how it happened, and why it happened.
> ★ Stories have a beginning, a middle, and an end.

Write a story about the picture below. Be sure to follow all the hints in the "Things to Think About" box. Give your story a title.

Name _____

Skill: Writing Stories

THINGS TO THINK ABOUT FOR EVERY STORY:

★ **Sentences begin with capitals and end with periods, question marks, or exclamation marks.**
★ **A paragraph contains a main idea and supporting details.**
★ **The first sentence of a paragraph should be indented.**
★ **Adjectives make stories more colorful and interesting.**
★ **A story tells who did what, when and where it was done, how it happened, and why it happened.**
★ **Stories have a beginning, a middle, and an end.**

Write a story about the picture below. Be sure to follow all the hints in the "Things to Think About" box. Give your story a title.

©1996 Kelley Wingate Publications   CD-3720

Name _____   Skill: Three Paragraph Stories

Putting Paragraphs Together
★ Each paragraph in a story contains a main idea and supporting details.
★ The opening paragraph gives the topic of the story. It should catch the interest of the reader.
★ The second paragraph gives more information about the topic of the story.
★ The last paragraph reviews the main idea and ends the story.

Use the information contained in this outline to write a three paragraph story. Use an extra sheet of paper if you need more space.

Title: <u>The School Fair</u>
Main Idea: I. Games to play
Details: A. relay races
                      B. ring toss
                      C. basketball throw

Main Idea: II. Food to eat
                      A. pizza
                      B. popcorn
                      C. candy

Main Idea: III. Love the fair
                      A. face painted
                      B. win prizes
                      C. run with friends

_____

_____

_____
_____
_____
_____
_____
_____
_____

©1996 Kelley Wingate Publications   CD-3720

Name _____   Skill: Three Paragraph Stories

Putting Paragraphs Together
★ Each paragraph in a story contains a main idea and supporting details.
★ The opening paragraph gives the topic of the story. It should catch the interest of the reader.
★ The second paragraph gives more information about the topic of the story.
★ The last paragraph reviews the main idea and ends the story.

Use the information contained in this outline to write a three paragraph story. Use an extra sheet of paper if you need more space.

Title: <u>Camping</u>
Main Idea: I. Get camping gear
Details: A. check tent
    B. test flashlights
    C. pack food

Main Idea: II. Set up camp
    A. find a spot
    B. pitch tent
    C. build campfire pit

Main Idea: III. Enjoy the trip
    A. take hikes
    B. go fishing
    C. cook over the fire

©1996 Kelley Wingate Publications   CD-3720

Name _____   Skill: Three Paragraph Stories

> **Putting Paragraphs Together**
> ★ Each paragraph in a story contains a main idea and supporting details.
> ★ The opening paragraph gives the topic of the story. It should catch the interest of the reader.
> ★ The second paragraph gives more information about the topic of the story.
> ★ The last paragraph reviews the main idea and ends the story.

Add your own details then use the information contained in this outline to write a three paragraph story. Use an extra sheet of paper if you need more space.

Title: Rub-A-Dub Dog
Main Idea: I. Getting ready
Details: A. fill tub with water
   B. get shampoo and towels
   C. _____

Main Idea: II. Bath time
   A. squirt the shampoo
   B. lather the dog
   C. _____

Main Idea: III. Clean and happy
   A. dry the dog with towels
   B. brush the fur
   C. _____

©1996 Kelley Wingate Publications   CD-3720

Name _____   Skill: Three Paragraph Stories

> **Putting Paragraphs Together**
> ★ Each paragraph in a story contains a main idea and supporting details.
> ★ The opening paragraph gives the topic of the story. It should catch the interest of the reader.
> ★ The second paragraph gives more information about the topic of the story.
> ★ The last paragraph reviews the main idea and ends the story.

Add your own details then use the information contained in this outline to write a three paragraph story. Use an extra sheet of paper if you need more space.

Title: <u>Painting the Porch</u>
Main Idea: I. Porch needed painting
Details: A. paint was peeling
                         B. looked shabby
                         C. _____

Main Idea: II. Worked all weekend
                         A. scraped off old paint
                         B. washed down the walls
                         C. _____

Main Idea: III. Looks like new
                         A. fresh bright paint
                         B. looks clean and nice
                         C. _____

_____

            _____

_____
_____
_____
_____
_____
_____
_____

Name _____   Skill: Three Paragraph Stories

Putting Paragraphs Together
★ Each paragraph in a story contains a main idea and supporting details.
★ The opening paragraph gives the topic of the story. It should catch the interest of the reader.
★ The second paragraph gives more information about the topic of the story.
★ The last paragraph reviews the main idea and ends the story.

Add your own details then use the information contained in this outline to write a three paragraph story. Use an extra sheet of paper if you need more space.

Title: <u>Visit to the Dentist</u>
Main Idea: I. Painful tooth
Details: A. bit into a candied apple
    B. _____
    C. _____

Main Idea: II. Called the dentist
    A. told nurse the problem
    B. _____
    C. _____

Main Idea: III. Saw the dentist
    A. took x-rays of my tooth
    B. _____
    C. _____

_____

_____
_____
_____
_____
_____
_____
_____

Name _____   Skill: Three Paragraph Stories

Putting Paragraphs Together
★ Each paragraph in a story contains a main idea and supporting details.
★ The opening paragraph gives the topic of the story. It should catch the interest of the reader.
★ The second paragraph gives more information about the topic of the story.
★ The last paragraph reviews the main idea and ends the story.

Add your own details then use the information contained in this outline to write a three paragraph story. Use an extra sheet of paper if you need more space.

Title: <u>The Science Project Contest</u>
Main Idea: I. Decide on a project
Details:
            A. _____
            B. _____
            C. _____

Main Idea: II. Find out the facts
            A. _____
            B. _____
            C. _____

Main Idea: III. Make the project
            A. _____
            B. _____
            C. _____

_____

        _____

_____
_____
_____
_____
_____
_____
_____

Name _____   Skill: Three Paragraph Stories

> **Putting Paragraphs Together**
> ★ Each paragraph in a story contains a main idea and supporting details.
> ★ The opening paragraph gives the topic of the story. It should catch the interest of the reader.
> ★ The second paragraph gives more information about the topic of the story.
> ★ The last paragraph reviews the main idea and ends the story.

Choose a topic and fill in the outline for a three paragraph story. Use an extra sheet of paper if you need more space.

Title: _____

Main Idea: I. _____

Details: A. _____
                          B. _____
                          C. _____

Main Idea: II. _____
                          A. _____
                          B. _____
                          C. _____

Main Idea: III. _____
                          A. _____
                          B. _____
                          C. _____

_____

_____

_____
_____
_____
_____
_____
_____
_____

Name _____ Skill: Three Paragraph Story Web

> **Putting Paragraphs Together**
> ★ Each paragraph in a story contains a main idea and supporting details.
> ★ The opening paragraph gives the topic of the story. It should catch the interest of the reader.
> ★ The second paragraph gives more information about the topic of the story.
> ★ The last paragraph reviews the main idea and ends the story.

Use the information given in the story web to write a three paragraph story. Title the story. Use an extra sheet of paper if you need more space.

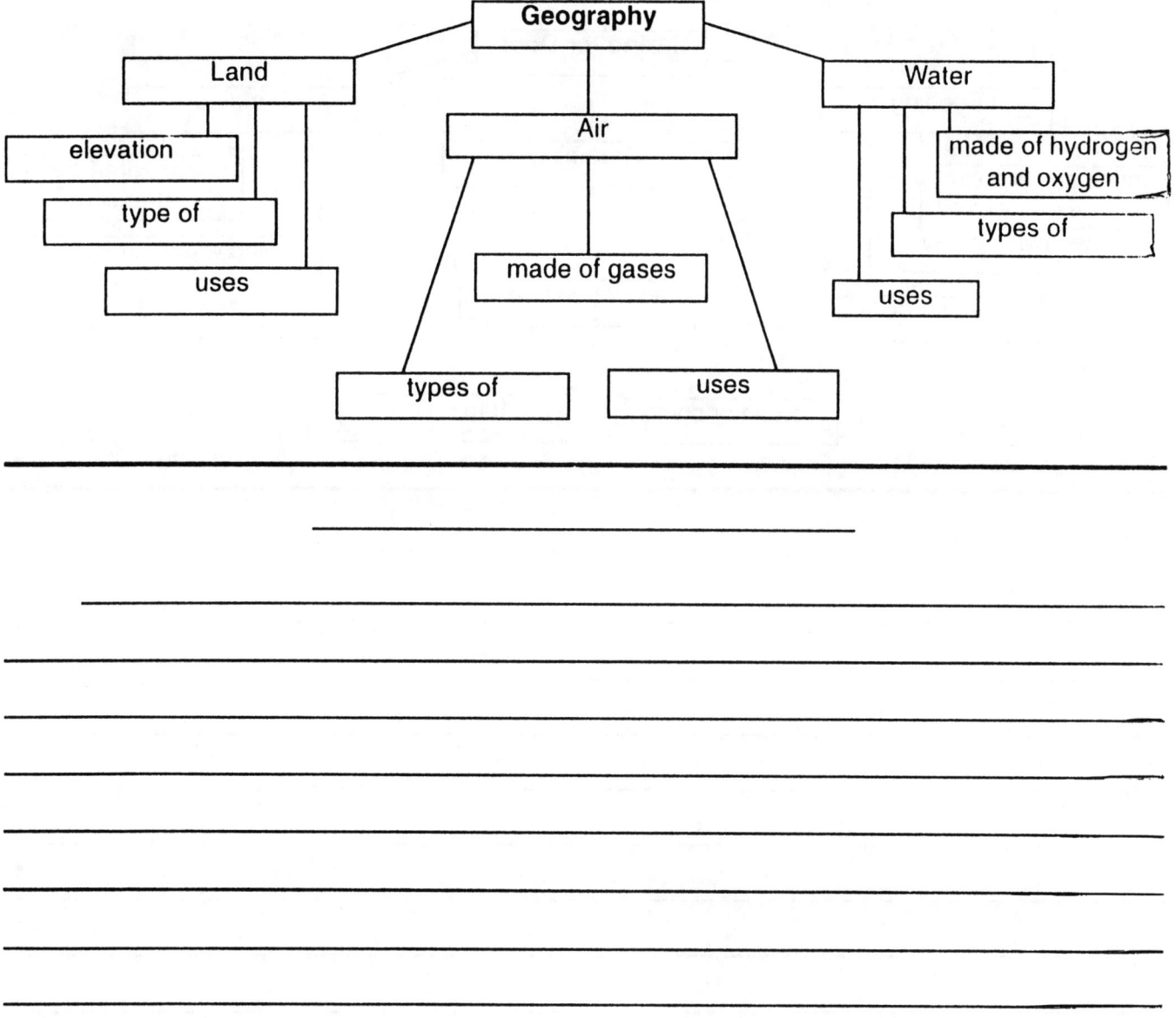

©1996 Kelley Wingate Publications CD-3720

Name _____ Skill: Three Paragraph Story Web

Putting Paragraphs Together
★ Each paragraph in a story contains a main idea and supporting details.
★ The opening paragraph gives the topic of the story. It should catch the interest of the reader.
★ The second paragraph gives more information about the topic of the story.
★ The last paragraph reviews the main idea and ends the story.

Use the information given in the story web to write a three paragraph story. Title the story. Use an extra sheet of paper if you need more space.

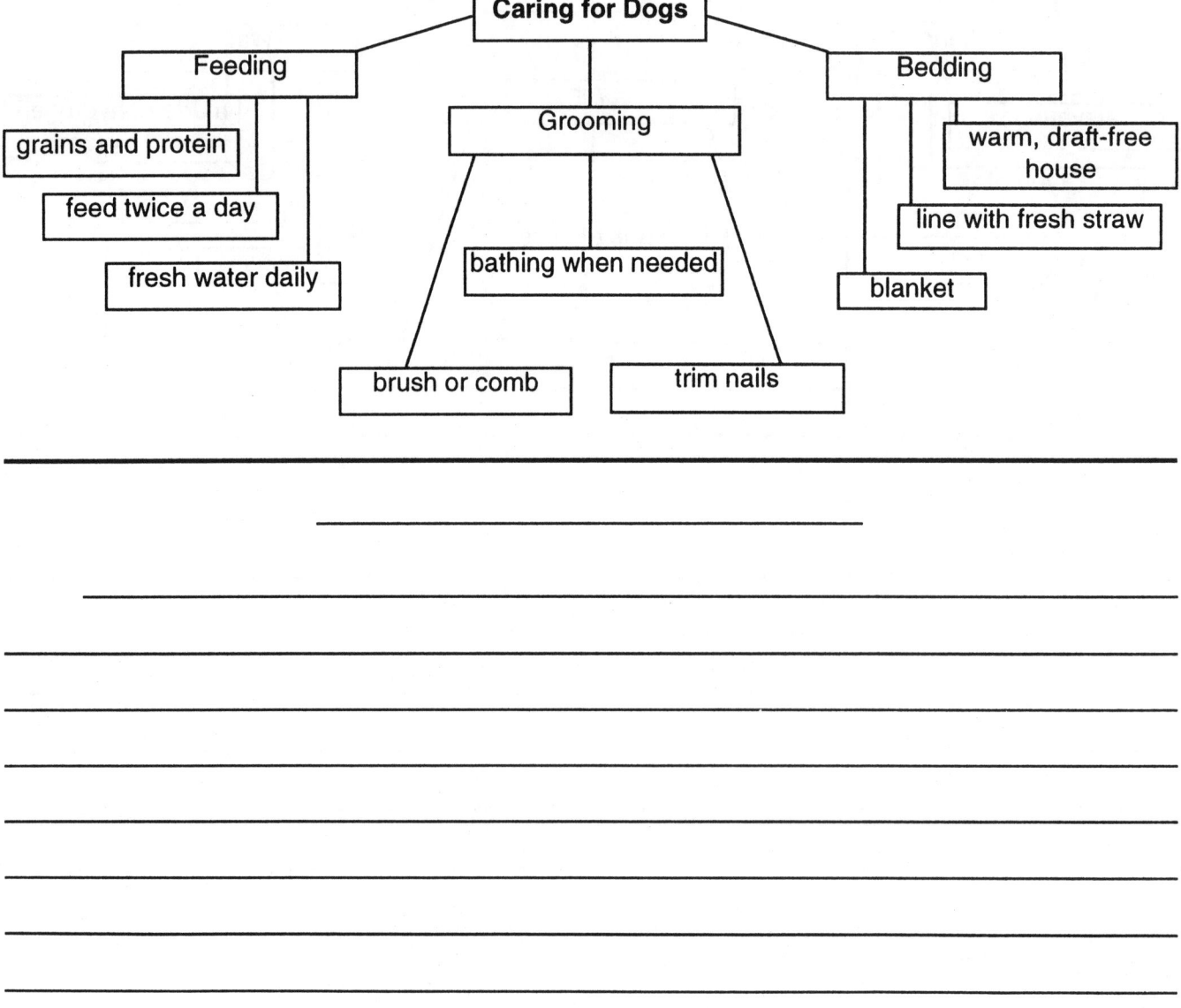

©1996 Kelley Wingate Publications

Name _____ Skill: Three Paragraph Story Web

> **Putting Paragraphs Together**
> ★ Each paragraph in a story contains a main idea and supporting details.
> ★ The opening paragraph gives the topic of the story. It should catch the interest of the reader.
> ★ The second paragraph gives more information about the topic of the story.
> ★ The last paragraph reviews the main idea and ends the story.

Finish filling in the details for each subheading. Use the information in the story web to write a three paragraph story. Title your story. Use an extra sheet of paper if you need more space.

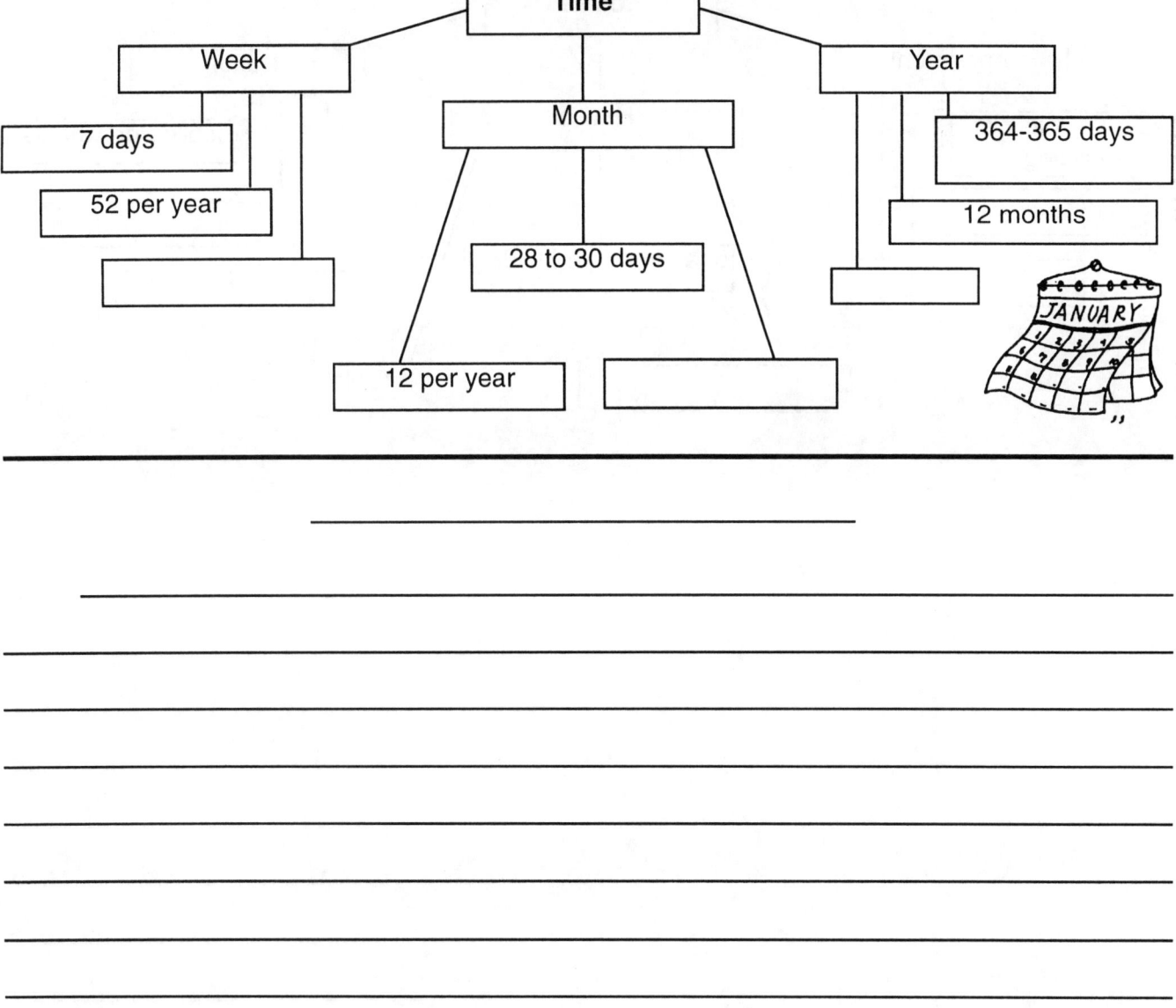

_____

_____
_____
_____
_____
_____
_____
_____
_____

©1996 Kelley Wingate Publications   CD-3720

Name _____   Skill: Three Paragraph Story Web

Putting Paragraphs Together
★ Each paragraph in a story contains a main idea and supporting details.
★ The opening paragraph gives the topic of the story. It should catch the interest of the reader.
★ The second paragraph gives more information about the topic of the story.
★ The last paragraph reviews the main idea and ends the story.

Finish filling in the details for each subheading. Use the information in the story web to write a three paragraph story. Title your story. Use an extra sheet of paper if you need more space.

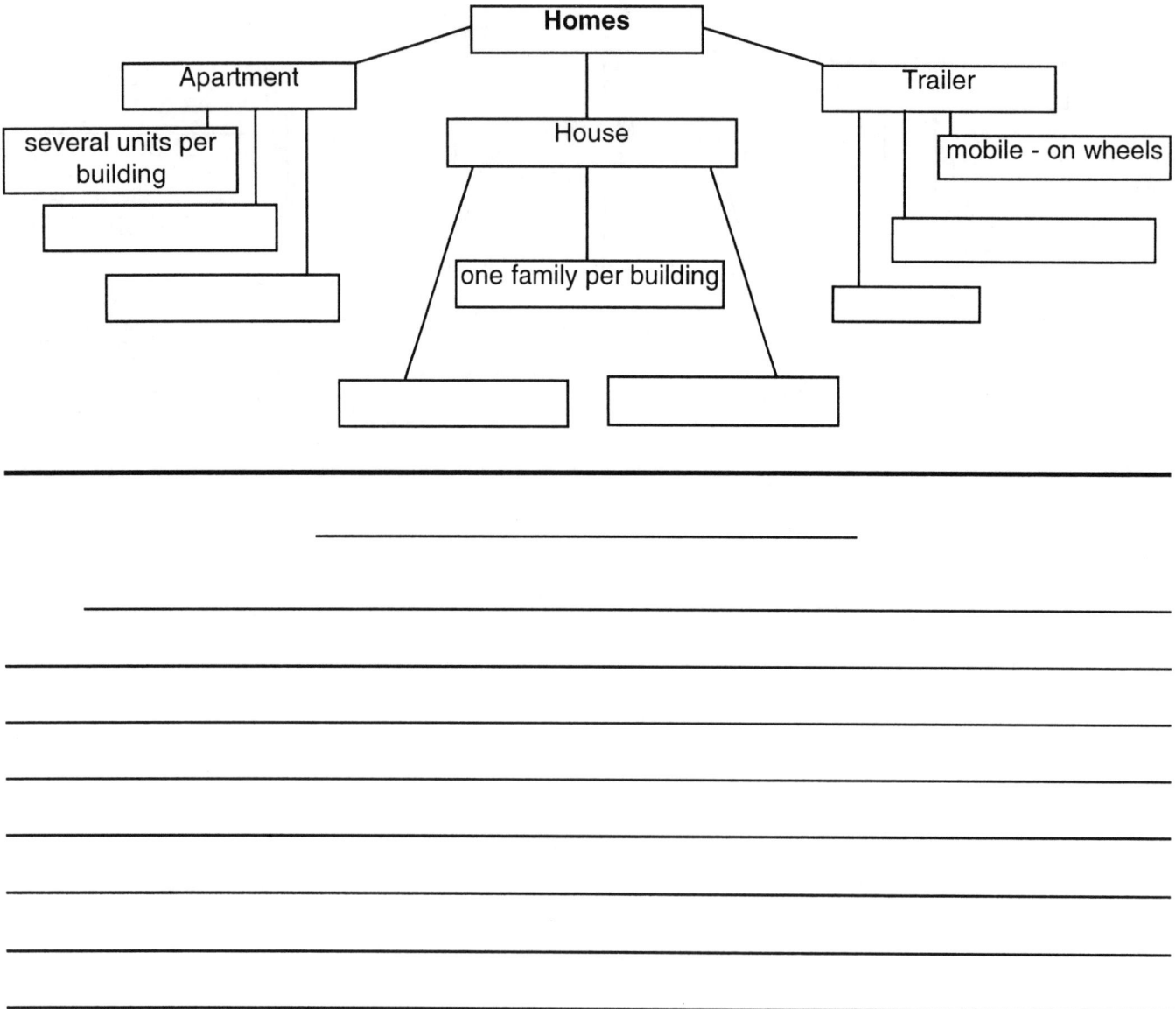

©1996 Kelley Wingate Publications   76   CD-3720

Name _____   Skill: Three Paragraph Story Web

Putting Paragraphs Together
★ Each paragraph in a story contains a main idea and supporting details.
★ The opening paragraph gives the topic of the story. It should catch the interest of the reader.
★ The second paragraph gives more information about the topic of the story.
★ The last paragraph reviews the main idea and ends the story.

Finish filling in the details for each subheading. Use the information in the story web to write a three paragraph story. Title your story. Use an extra sheet of paper if you need more space.

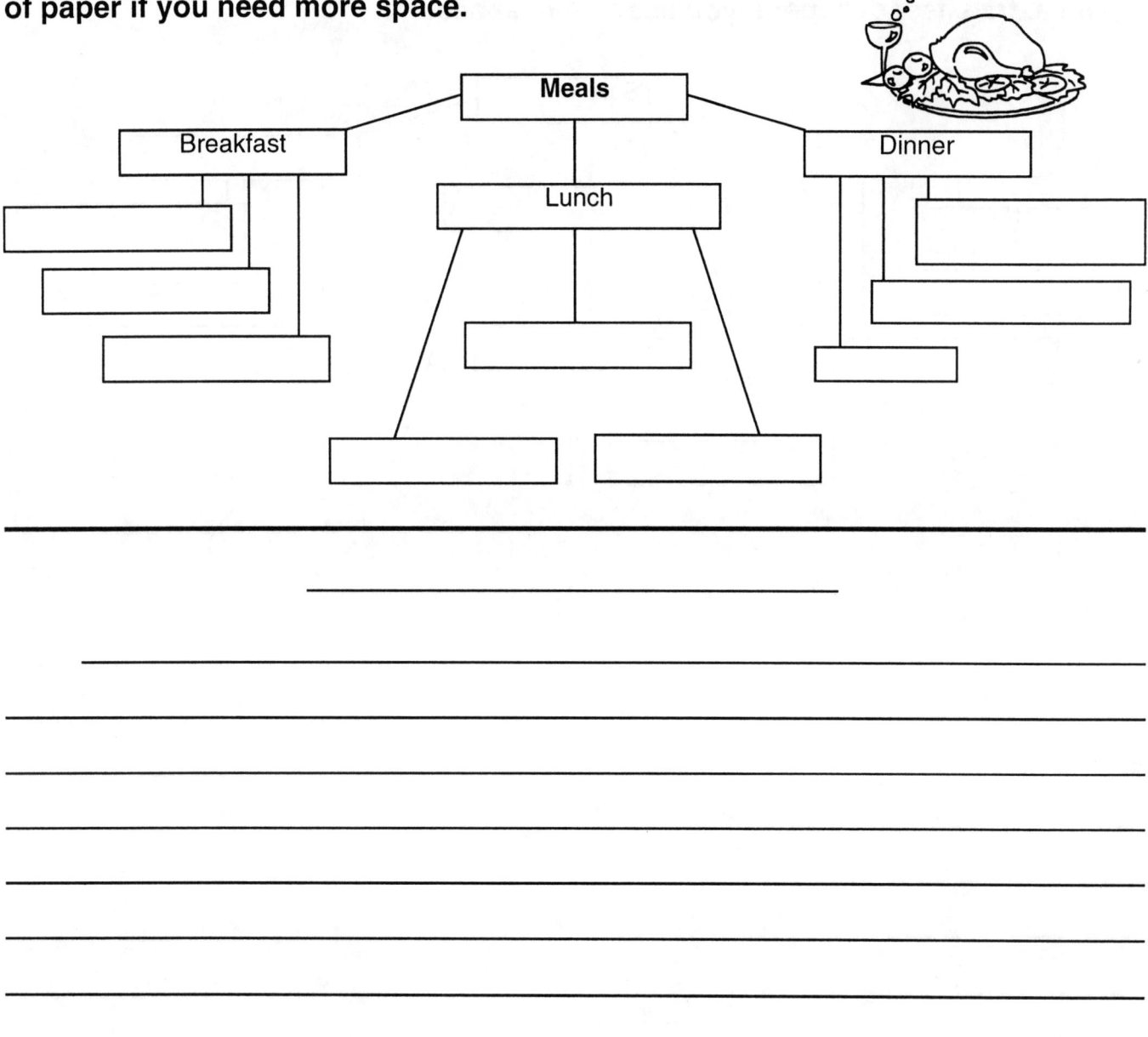

_____

_____

_____
_____
_____
_____
_____
_____
_____

©1996 Kelley Wingate Publications   CD-3720

Name _____   Skill: Three Paragraph Story Web

Putting Paragraphs Together
Each paragraph in a story contains a main idea and supporting details.
The opening paragraph gives the topic of the story. It should catch the interest of the reader.
The second paragraph gives more information about the topic of the story.
The last paragraph reviews the main idea and ends the story.

Fill in the subheadings and details to complete the story web. Use the information in the story web to write a three paragraph story. Title your story. Use an extra sheet of paper if you need more space.

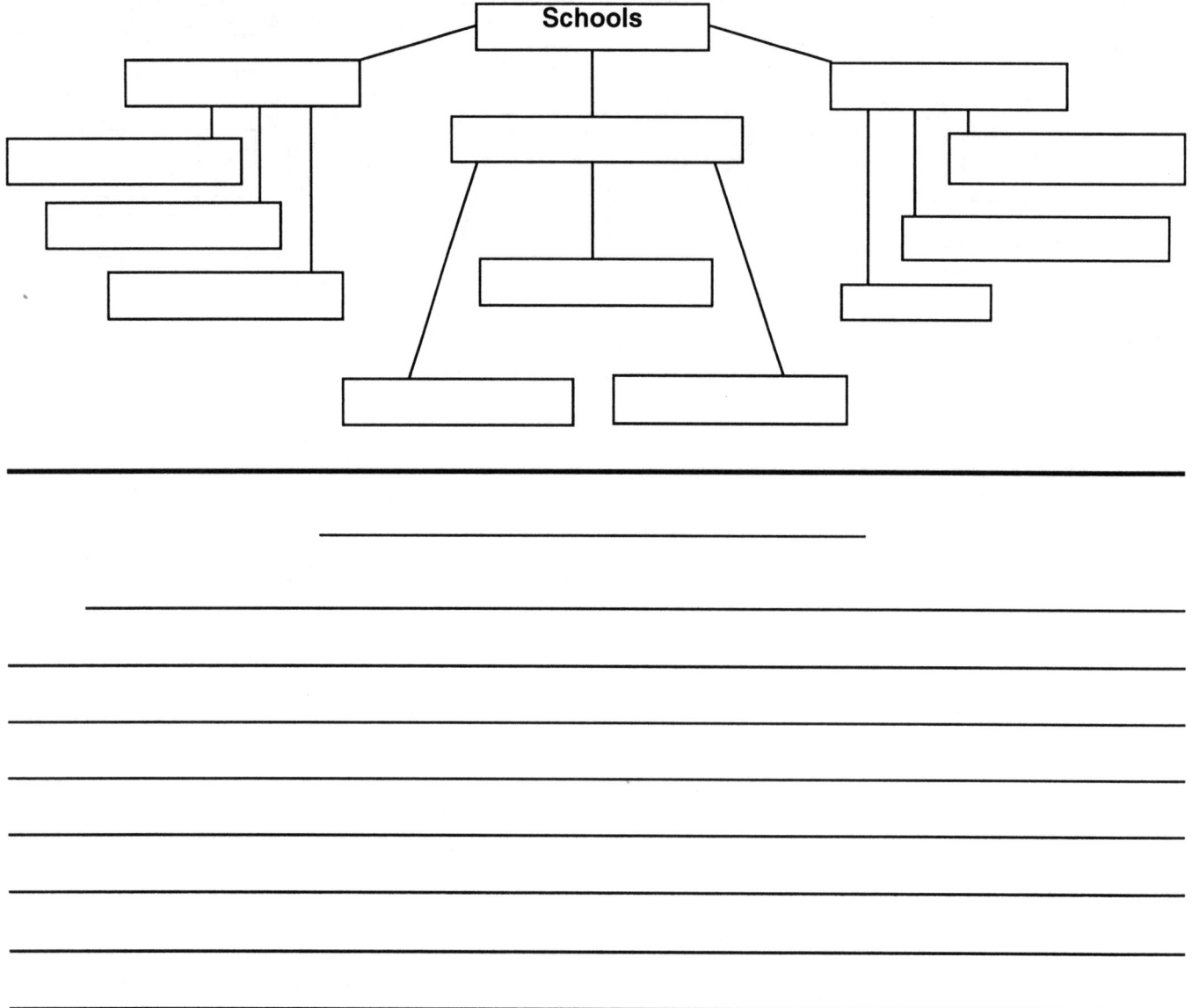

©1996 Kelley Wingate Publications   CD-3720

Name _____   Skill: Three Paragraph Story Web

> **Putting Paragraphs Together**
> Each paragraph in a story contains a main idea and supporting details.
> The opening paragraph gives the topic of the story. It should catch the interest of the reader.
> The second paragraph gives more information about the topic of the story.
> The last paragraph reviews the main idea and ends the story.

Fill in the main heading, subheading, and details to complete the story web below. Use the information in the story web to write a three paragraph story. Title your story. Use an extra sheet of paper if you need more space.

©1996 Kelley Wingate Publications   CD-3720

Name _____   Skill: Writing Reports

> **A report gives facts in an orderly and clear manner.**

Use the information contained in this outline to write a report. Use an extra sheet of paper if you need more space.

Subject: Balanced Diet
Main Idea: I. Necessary for good health
Details: A. builds strong bones
                  B. strengthens muscles
                  C. provides energy
Main Idea: II. Five food groups
                  A. protein
                  B. milk products
                  C. grains
                  D. fruits
                  E. vegetables
Main Idea: III. Servings per day
                  A. two proteins
                  B. three milk products
                  C. three grains
                  D. three fruits

_____

_____
_____
_____
_____
_____
_____
_____
_____
_____
_____
_____

Name _____   Skill: Writing Reports

> **A report gives facts in an orderly and clear manner.**

Use the information contained in this outline to write a report. Use an extra sheet of paper if you need more space.

Subject: Layers of the Earth
Main Idea: I. Crust
Details:
    A. outer layer
    B. solid and thin
    C. 5 - 30 miles thick

Main Idea: II. Mantle
    A. middle layer
    B. liquid rock under heat and pressure
    C. 1800 miles thick

Main Idea: III. Core
    A. center of the Earth
    B. melted and solid iron and nickel
    C. 4,400 miles thick

_____

_____
_____
_____
_____
_____
_____
_____
_____
_____

©1996 Kelley Wingate Publications

Name _____ Skill: Writing Reports

A report gives facts in an orderly and clear manner.

Use the information contained in this outline to write a report. Use an extra sheet of paper if you need more space.

Subject: Transportation
Main Idea: I. Planes
Details: A. gliders
                B. small private
                C. commercial

Main Idea: II. Trains
                A. freight
                B. passenger
                C. express

Main Idea: III. Ships
                A. freighters
                B. cargo
                C. cruise liners

©1996 Kelley Wingate Publications   CD-3720

Name _____ Skill: Writing Reports

| A report gives facts in an orderly and clear manner. |

Use the information contained in this outline to write a report. Use an extra sheet of paper if you need more space.

Subject: Bodies In Space
Main Idea: I. Planets
Details: A. some are rocks
                    B. some are gases
                    C. orbit a star

Main Idea: II. Satellites
                    A. range in size (dust to almost planet size)
                    B. made of rock or dust
                    C. orbit a planet

Main Idea: III. Stars
                    A. burning gases
                    B. millions in space
                    C. many different colors depending on temperature

_____

_____
_____
_____
_____
_____
_____
_____
_____
_____

Name _____   Skill: Writing Reports

> **A report gives facts in an orderly and clear manner.**

Fill in the details and use the information contained in this outline to write a report. Use an extra sheet of paper if you need more space.

Subject: Storms
Main Idea: I. Thunder storms
Details: A. _____
                         B. _____
                         C. _____

Main Idea: II. Tornadoes
                         A. _____
                         B. _____
                         C. _____

Main Idea: III. Hurricanes
                         A. _____
                         B. _____
                         C. _____

_____

_____
_____
_____
_____
_____
_____
_____
_____
_____
_____

Name _____   Skill: Writing Reports

> A report gives facts in an orderly and clear manner.

Choose a topic and write the information in this outline. Use the information to write a report. Use an extra sheet of paper if you need more space.

Subject: _____
Main Idea: I. _____
Details: A. _____
                              B. _____
                              C. _____

Main Idea: II. _____
                              A. _____
                              B. _____
                              C. _____

Main Idea: III. _____
                              A. _____
                              B. _____
                              C. _____

_____

_____
_____
_____
_____
_____
_____
_____
_____
_____
_____

Name _____   Skill: Point of View

> The **first person point of view** tells a story as if the narrator were a part of it. This view uses the words "I", "me", or "we".
> The **third person point of view** tells the story as if the narrator were watching it happen. This view uses the words "he", "she", "they", or "them".

This story is written from the first person point of view. Rewrite the story, changing it to the third person point of view. Add your own ending.

The Rescue

My friends and I were at the beach. We were laying in the sun and watching the sea gulls overhead. It was a beautiful, relaxing day. I thought I heard a faint cry for help. I listened closely and looked around the beach. I heard it again, but saw nothing unusual on the beach. I looked out at the water and spotted a head bobbing in the waves. I....

_____
_____
_____
_____
_____
_____
_____
_____
_____
_____
_____
_____
_____
_____
_____
_____

Name _____   Skill: Point of View

> The **first person point of view** tells a story as if the narrator were a part of it. This view uses the words "I", "me", or "we".
> The **third person point of view** tells the story as if the narrator were watching it happen. This view uses the words "he", "she", "they", or "them".

This story is written from the first person point of view. Rewrite the story, changing it to the third person point of view. Add your own ending.

<u>Hang on for Dear Life</u>

    I had never ridden a horse before, and I was not sure I wanted to now. My friend, Susie, was sure I would love it. I climbed in the saddle and took the reins in my hands. Susie was beside me on her horse. We started off slowly. I began to relax and almost enjoyed myself. The rocking of the saddle was rather pleasant after all. Just then a rabbit darted out in front of us. My horse....

_____
_____
_____
_____
_____
_____
_____
_____
_____
_____
_____
_____
_____
_____

Name _____   Skill: Point of View

> The **first person point of view** tells a story as if the narrator were a part of it. This view uses the words "I", "me", or "we".
> The **third person point of view** tells the story as if the narrator were watching it happen. This view uses the words "he", "she", "they", or "them".

This story is written from the first person point of view. Rewrite the story, changing it to the third person point of view. Add your own ending.

<u>Gotcha!</u>

    I plopped down on my bed and took off my slippers. It had been a very long day and I was totally worn out. I yawned tiredly and pulled back the covers. That pillow looked so inviting! I could hardly keep my eyes open any more. I sat on the edge of the bed and reached over to turn off the lamp. Just as the light went out I felt something grab my ankle! It pulled me....

_____
_____
_____
_____
_____
_____
_____
_____
_____
_____
_____
_____
_____
_____

Name _____   Skill: Point of View

> The **first person point of view** tells a story as if the narrator were a part of it. This view uses the words "I", "me", or "we".
> The **third person point of view** tells the story as if the narrator were watching it happen. This view uses the words "he", "she", "they", or "them".

This story is written from the third person point of view. Rewrite the story, changing it to the first person point of view. Add your own ending.

<u>Down the Drain</u>

    It was the day after Colleen's eleventh birthday. Her parents had given her a beautiful gold ring. Collen thought it was the prettiest ring she had ever seen. She was so proud of it that she had worn it to school that day to show it to her friends.
    When Colleen got home from school she went into the kitchen and sat near the window to watch her ring sparkle in the sunlight. Her mom asked her to help with dinner by washing and cutting the carrots. Colleen turned on the water and began to rinse the carrots. Just when she was almost finished, her ring....

Name _____   Skill: Point of View

> The **first person point of view** tells a story as if the narrator were a part of it. This view uses the words "I", "me", or "we".
> The **third person point of view** tells the story as if the narrator were watching it happen. This view uses the words "he", "she", "they", or "them".

This story is written from the third person point of view. Rewrite the story, changing it to the first person point of view. Add your own ending.

The Frog Jumping Contest

    Hank and his brother James were spending the summer at their Grandmother's farm. They had just met two boys, Stan and Jeff, from a nearby farm. Stan and Jeff had caught four big frogs down by a nearby pond.

    "I have an idea," said Stan. "Let's have a frog jumping contest. We will each choose a frog and put it down on the grass. The frog that jumps past that big old oak tree first will be the winner."

    Each boy chose a frog and lined it up. The race began. Hank's frog was in the lead when suddenly....

_____
_____
_____
_____
_____
_____
_____
_____
_____
_____
_____
_____
_____

Name _____   Skill: Point of View

> The **first person point of view** tells a story as if the narrator were a part of it. This view uses the words "I", "me", or "we".
> The **third person point of view** tells the story as if the narrator were watching it happen. This view uses the words "he", "she", "they", or "them".

This story is written from the third person point of view. Rewrite the story, changing it to the first person point of view. Add your own ending.

At the Top

    Jill had been waiting all winter for this warm sunny morning. She loved to go mountain climbing, and today would be the first time she would go this year. She packed her lunch, put on her climbing boots, and was off. It would be wonderful to sit on the mountain and eat her lunch. The view was always breathtaking! Jill was daydreaming so much she forgot to pay close attention to what she was doing. She had nearly reached the top when she felt loose gravel sliding beneath her feet. Jill hit the ground and began to slide toward a rocky ledge. She frantically grabbed at ....

Name _____   Skill: Character Webs

Actions tell us about characters.

Characters tell us about themselves by the way they act. These actions make something happen in a story. When we understand characters and their actions, we understand the story.

Goldilocks and the Three Bears

Character
Goldilocks

Action
She went into the house when no one was home.

Action
She slept in Baby Bear's bed.

Action
She ate the bears' food.

What the action tells us
She was not very polite.

What the action tells us
She was tired and didn't care if she got caught trespassing.

What the action tells us
She was hungry and did not respect other people's property

Use the information from the chart to write a paragraph about Goldilocks.

_____
_____
_____
_____
_____
_____

Name _____   Skill: Character Webs

Actions tell us about characters.

Characters tell us about themselves by the way they act. These actions make something happen in a story. When we understand characters and their actions, we understand the story.

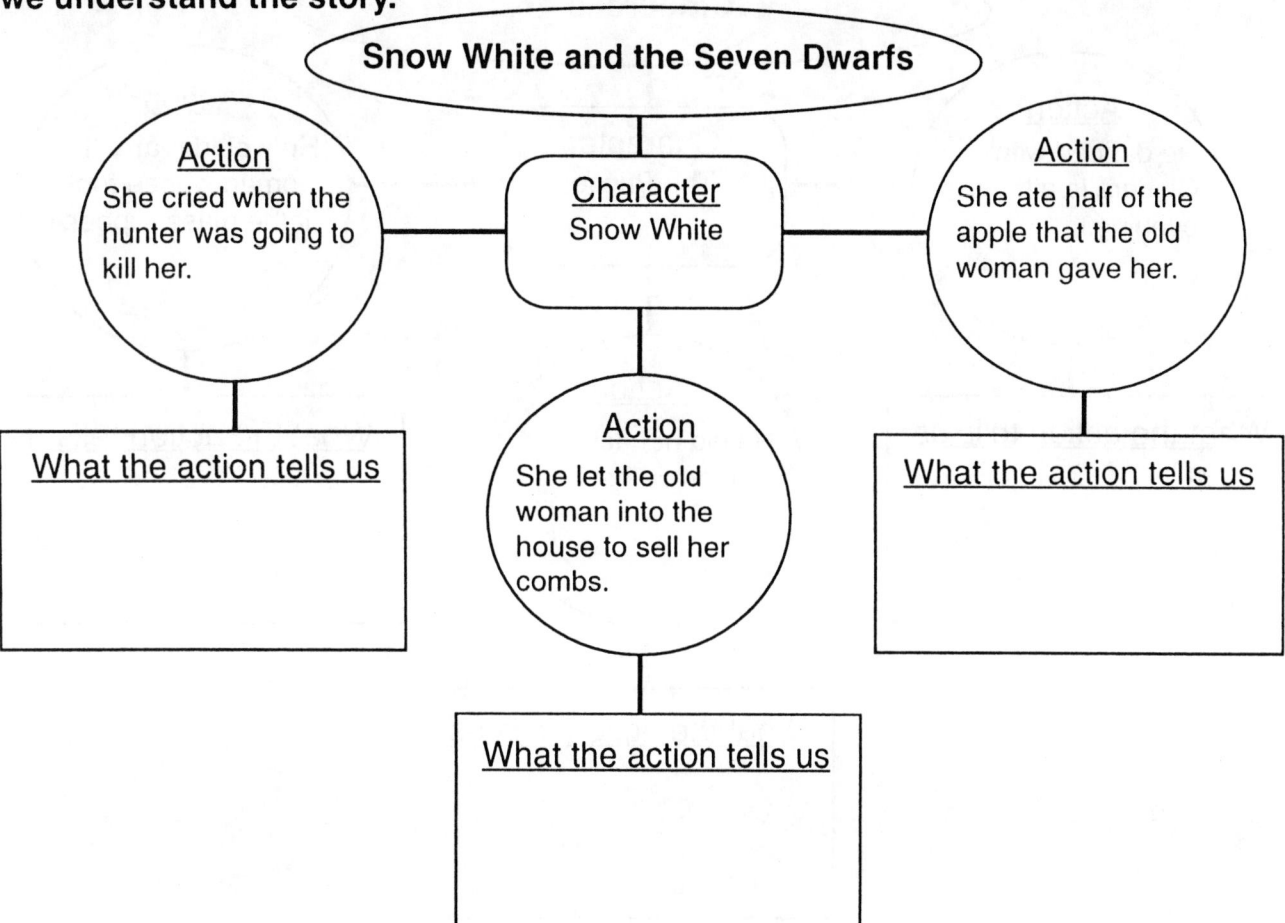

Complete the chart. Use the information to write a paragraph about the Queen.

_____
_____
_____
_____
_____
_____
_____

Name _____ Skill: Character Webs

Actions tell us about characters.

Characters tell us about themselves by the way they act. These actions make something happen in a story. When we understand characters and their actions, we understand the story.

Cinderella

Action
He danced with Cinderella all evening.

Character
The Prince

Action
He would marry the woman whose foot fit the glass slipper.

Action
He did not ask Cinderella her name.

What the action tells us

What the action tells us

What the action tells us

Complete the chart. Use the information to write a paragraph about the Prince.

_____
_____
_____
_____
_____
_____

©1996 Kelley Wingate Publications

Name _____   Skill: Character Webs

Actions tell us about characters.

Characters tell us about themselves by the way they act. These actions make something happen in a story. When we understand characters and their actions, we understand the story.

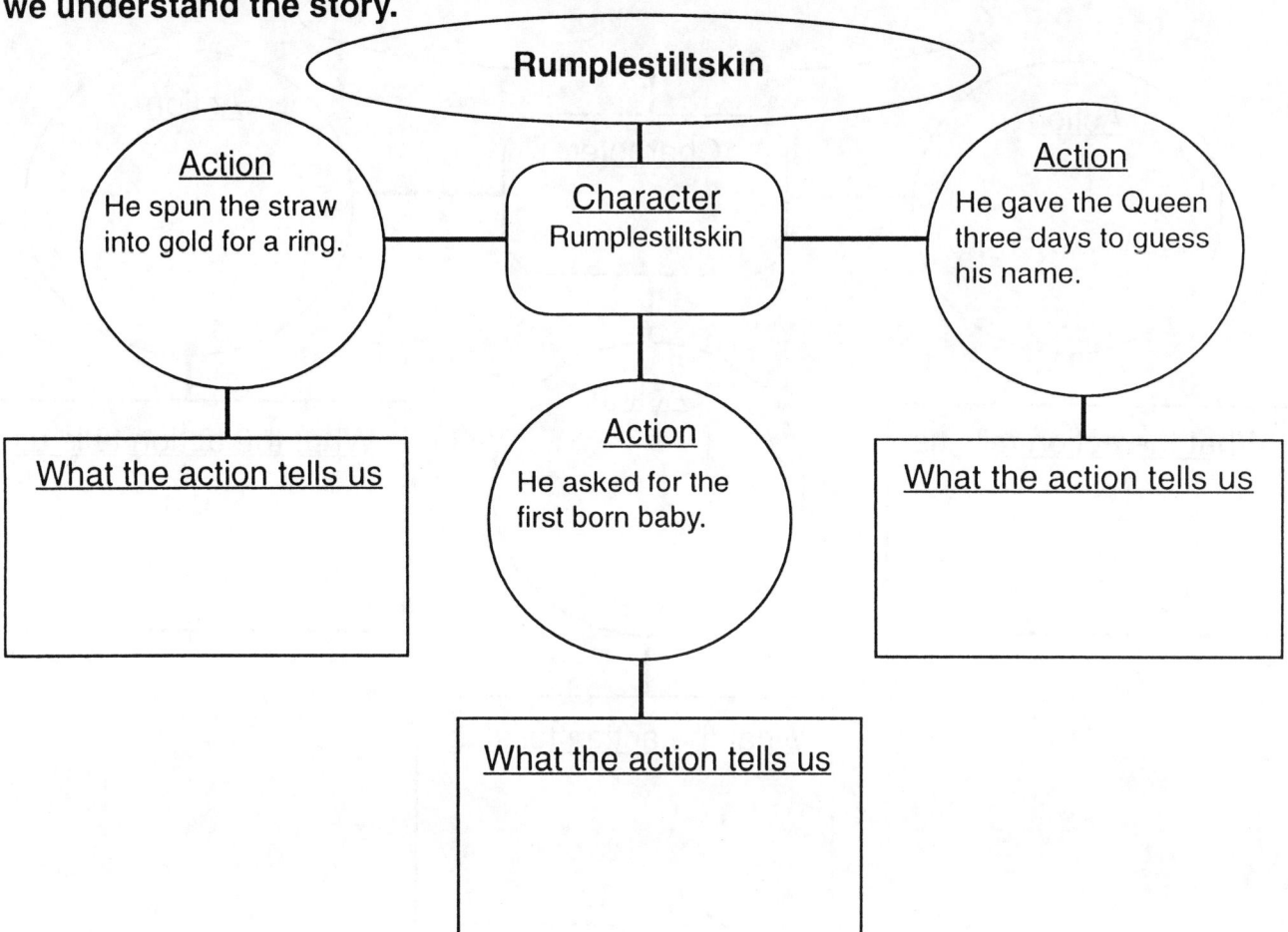

Complete the chart. Use the information to write a paragraph about Rumplestiltskin.

_____
_____
_____
_____
_____
_____

Name _____   Skill: Character Webs

Actions tell us about characters.

Characters tell us about themselves by the way they act. These actions make something happen in a story. When we understand characters and their actions, we understand the story.

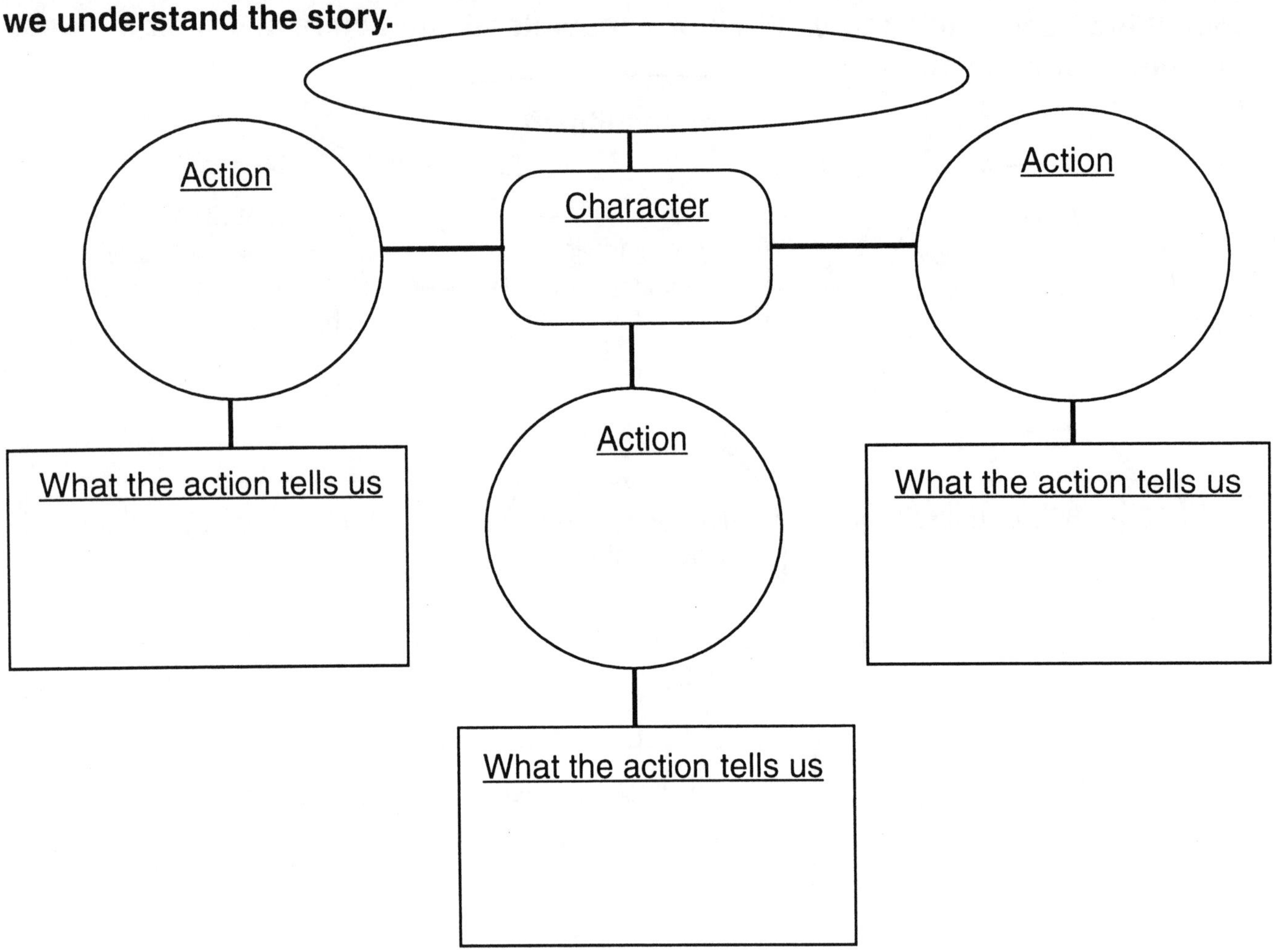

- (empty oval)
- Action
- Character
- Action
- Action
- What the action tells us
- What the action tells us
- What the action tells us

Complete the chart for a character from a story you have read. Use the information to write a paragraph about that character.

_____
_____
_____
_____
_____
_____

©1996 Kelley Wingate Publications

Name _____   Skill: Book Reports - Story Elements

Book Report

1. Title:

2. Author:

3. Name 2 characters in this book. Write a sentence about each one.

   A. _____ _____
   _____

   B. _____ _____
   _____

4. Tell where this story takes place. Write a sentence to describe the setting.
   _____
   _____

5. What is the problem in this story?
   _____
   _____
   _____
   _____

6. How is the problem solved?
   _____
   _____
   _____
   _____

Name _____

Skill: Book Reports - Story Elements

About This Book

Characters

_____
_____
_____

_____ (title)

By: _____ (author)

(end)

(middle)

(beginning)

Name _____   Skill: Book Reports - Story Elements

Book Review

Title: _____

Author: _____

1. Retell the story in your own words. Be sure to include the characters, setting, beginning, middle, and end.

_____
_____
_____
_____
_____
_____
_____
_____
_____

2. Tell what you liked most about this story. Tell why and give examples from the book.

_____
_____
_____
_____
_____
_____
_____
_____
_____

©1996 Kelley Wingate Publications

Name _____   Skill: Book Reports - Fiction Books

Book Report

Title: _____

Author: _____

Where did this story take place? _____
_____

1. Compare and contrast the main character with yourself.

contrast	compare	compare

2. Tell what you liked or didn't like about the main character. Tell why and give examples from the book.

Name _____   Skill: Book Reports - Fiction Books

_____
(Title)

_____
(Author)

_____
(Date Published)

My favorite scene from the book.

WHO? _____
_____

WHAT? _____
_____
_____
_____
_____
_____

WHERE? _____
_____
_____
_____

WHEN? _____
_____

WHY? _____
_____
_____
_____
_____
_____

Name: _____   Skill: Book Reports - Nonfiction Books

Book Review

Title: _____

Author: _____

Date published: _____

Subject of the book: _____

Review of the book: _____
_____
_____
_____
_____
_____
_____

Interesting facts I learned from this book: _____
_____
_____
_____
_____
_____
_____

What I would like to know more about: _____
_____
_____

©1996 Kelley Wingate Publications   CD-3720

Name _____ Skill: Book Reports - Biography

Who's in the News?

Title: _____

Author: _____

Date published: _____

Who this book is about: _____

Why is this person important? _____
_____
_____
_____

What interesting things did this person do? _____
_____
_____
_____
_____
_____

How did this person affect history? _____
_____
_____
_____
_____
_____

How do you feel about this person? Why? _____
_____
_____
_____
_____

Name_____ Assignment: _____

Writing Award

_____

receives this award for

_____

Keep up the great work!

_____ _____
signed   date

Writing Whiz!

_____

receives this award for

_____

Great Job!

_____ _____
signed   date

Wonderful Writing!

_____

receives this award for

_____

Keep up the great work!

_____   _____

signed   date

All Star Writer

_____

is a Writing All Star!

_____

You are terrific!

_____   _____

signed   date

Answer Key

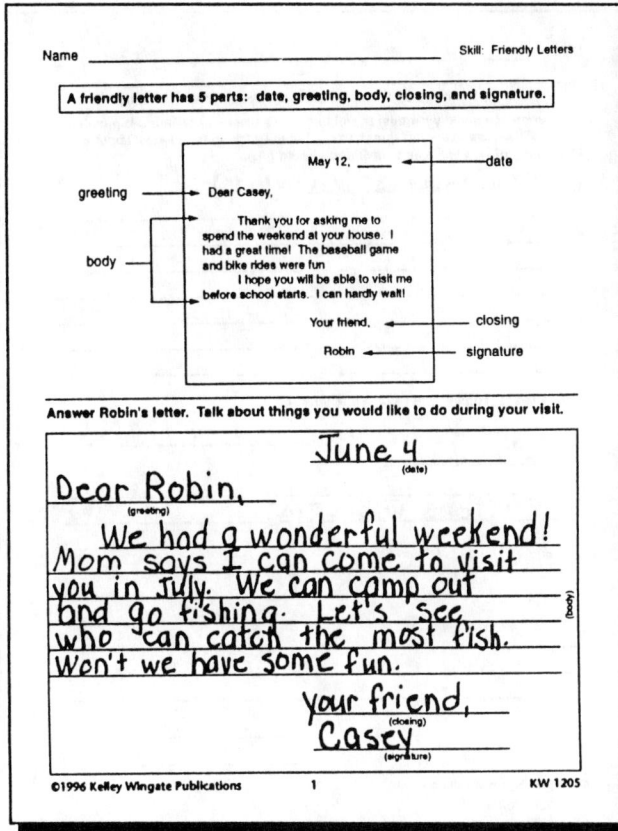
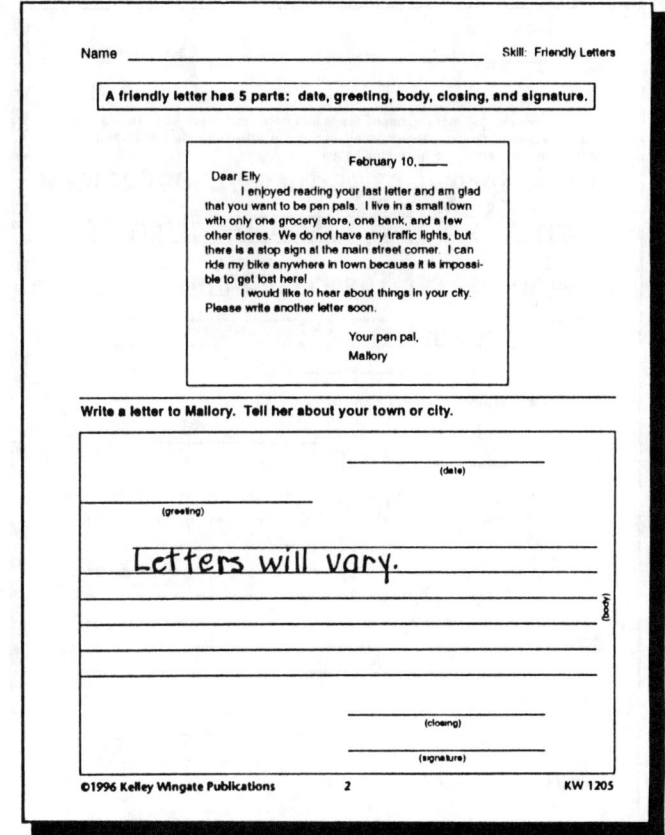

Answer Key

Page 5 — Skill: Friendly Letters

A friendly letter has 5 parts: date, greeting, body, closing, and signature.

1. You have decided that you might like to be a veterinarian one day. You have many questions about the job and have decided to write to a veterinarian and find out more. Write your questions below.

   1. How long does it take to become a veterinarian?
   2. What is a good school to attend?
   3. What is your favorite animal?
   4. Do you have a pet?

2. Use the questions to write your letter.

   Letters will vary.

Page 6 — Skill: Friendly Letters

A friendly letter has 5 parts: date, greeting, body, closing, and signature.

1. You want to invite your best friend to go on a weekend camping trip with your family. There are many fun things to do, but your friend is not sure about going. Make a list of reasons why your friend should go.

   1. (Statements will vary)
   2.
   3.
   4.

2. Use the reasons you listed to write your letter.

   Letters will vary.

Page 7 — Skill: Friendly Letters

A friendly letter has 5 parts: date, greeting, body, closing, and signature.

1. Choose a person to write to. List some of the things you want to say.

   1. (Statements will vary)
   2.
   3.
   4.

2. Use the list to write your letter.

   Letters will vary.

Page 8 — Skill: Writing Paragraphs

A paragraph contains a main idea and supporting details.

Every paragraph has one main idea. The main idea is called the topic sentence. It is usually the first sentence in the paragraph. The other sentences are details that tell more about the main idea. The last sentence retells the main idea.

1. Read over the information given below.

   Title of paragraph: Making Rain
   Main Idea: We made rain in my science class today.
   Details:
   1. First we froze a metal pie pan of water.
   2. Next we heated another pan of water until it steamed.
   3. We held the frozen water pie pan over the steam.
   4. When the steam touched it, water formed on the frozen pie pan and fell like rain.

   Retell Main Idea: Making rain was easy and fun.

2. Use the above information to write a paragraph. Write the main idea, add the details, then retell the main idea. Indent the first sentence. Use capitals and periods. Remember to give the paragraph a title.

   Making Rain

   We made rain in my science class today. First we froze a metal pie pan that was full of water. Next we heated another pan of water until it steamed. We held the frozen pie pan over the steam. When the steam touched it, water formed on the frozen pie pan and fell like rain. Making rain was easy and fun.

Answer Key

(Page 9) Skill: Writing Paragraphs

A paragraph contains a main idea and supporting details.

Every paragraph has one main idea. The main idea is called the topic sentence. It is usually the first sentence in the paragraph. The other sentences are details that tell more about the main idea. The last sentence retells the main idea.

1. Read over the information given below.

Title of paragraph: Shopping for a New Jacket

Main Idea: Mom and I went to the mall to buy a new jacket.

Details:
1. First we went to my favorite store.
2. I found six jackets that I really liked.
3. I tried on each jacket and looked in the mirror.
4. Mom and I agreed on which one we liked best.
5. We bought the jacket.

Retell Main Idea: My Mom and I picked out a new a jacket for me.

2. Use these sentences to write a paragraph. Write the main idea, add the details, then retell the main idea. Indent the first sentence. Use capitals and periods. Remember to give the paragraph a title.

Paragraphs will vary.

(Page 10) Skill: Writing Paragraphs

A paragraph contains a main idea and supporting details.

Every paragraph has one main idea. The main idea is called the topic sentence. It is usually the first sentence in the paragraph. The other sentences are details that tell more about the main idea. The last sentence retells the main idea.

Look at the title and main idea of the paragraph. Write your own details.

Title of paragraph: Birthdays Are Special

Main Idea: At my house, birthdays are special.

Details:
1. (details will vary)
2.
3.
4.

Retell Main Idea: I can hardly wait for my birthday!

2. Use these sentences to write a paragraph. Write the main idea, add the details, then retell the main idea. Indent the first sentence. Use capitals and periods. Remember to give the paragraph a title.

Paragraphs will vary.

(Page 11) Skill: Writing Paragraphs

A paragraph contains a main idea and supporting details.

Every paragraph has one main idea. The main idea is called the topic sentence. It is usually the first sentence in the paragraph. The other sentences are details that tell more about the main idea. The last sentence retells the main idea.

1. Look at the title and main idea of the paragraph. Write your own details.

Title of paragraph: Going to a Movie

Main Idea: I love to go to the movie theater on Saturday.

Details:
1. (details will vary)
2.
3.
4.

Retell Main Idea: Going to a movie makes Saturday a special day.

2. Use these sentences to write a paragraph. Write the main idea, add the details, then retell the main idea. Indent the first sentence. Use capitals and periods. Remember to give the paragraph a title.

Paragraphs will vary.

(Page 12) Skill: Writing Paragraphs

A paragraph contains a main idea and supporting details.

Every paragraph has one main idea. The main idea is called the topic sentence. It is usually the first sentence in the paragraph. The other sentences are details that tell more about the main idea. The last sentence retells the main idea.

1. Choose an idea for your paragraph. Write the title, main idea, and details. Retell the main idea at the end.

Title of paragraph: (answers will vary)

Main Idea:

Details:
1.
2.
3.
4.

Retell Main Idea:

2. Use the above information to write a paragraph. Write the main idea, add the details, then retell the main idea. Indent the first sentence. Use capitals and periods. Remember to give the paragraph a title.

Paragraphs will vary.

Answer Key

Worksheet 1 (p. 13) — Skill: Persuasive Paragraphs

A paragraph contains a main idea and supporting details.

Some paragraphs are written to persuade, or change the way people think. These paragraphs have a main idea and supporting details.

1. You must convince your parents to let you have a party. Ask them, give your reasons, then ask again.

- **Title:** The Party
- **Question:** May I have a party this Saturday afternoon?
- **Reasons:**
  1. I will invite only people you know.
  2. I will clean the house before and after the party.
  3. I will fix all of the snacks myself.
  4. We will follow all of the house rules.
- **Ask again:** Is it all right with you if I have a party this Saturday?

2. Use the above information to write a paragraph. Write the main idea, add the details, then retell the main idea. Indent the first sentence. Use capitals and periods. Remember to give the paragraph a title.

> **The Party**
>
> May I have a party this Saturday afternoon? I will invite only people you know. I will clean the house before and after the party. I will fix all of the snacks myself. We will follow all of the house rules. Is it all right with you if I have a party this Saturday?

Worksheet 2 (p. 14) — Skill: Persuasive Paragraphs

1. You must convince your mom to make pancakes for breakfast. Ask her, give your reasons, then ask again.

- **Title:** Pancakes for Breakfast
- **Question:** Will you make pancakes for breakfast, Mom?
- **Reasons:**
  1. I will help you cook them.
  2. I will wash the dishes after breakfast.
  3. We haven't had them in a long time.
  4. You make the best pancakes I've ever eaten.
- **Ask again:** May we have pancakes for breakfast this morning?

2. *Paragraphs will vary.*

Worksheet 3 (p. 15) — Skill: Persuasive Paragraphs

1. You must convince your dad to let you take karate lessons. Ask him, give your reasons, then ask again.

- **Title:** Karate Lessons
- **Question:** May I _____
- **Reasons:** (answers will vary)
- **Ask again:**

2. *Paragraphs will vary.*

Worksheet 4 (p. 16) — Skill: Persuasive Paragraphs

1. You must convince your mom to let you stay at a friend's house tonight. Ask her, give your reasons, then ask again.

- **Title:**
- **Question:** May I
- **Reasons:** (answers will vary)
- **Ask again:**

2. *Paragraphs will vary.*

Answer Key

Page 17 — Skill: Persuasive Paragraphs

A paragraph contains a main idea and supporting details.

Some paragraphs are written to persuade, or change the way people think. These paragraphs have a main idea and supporting details.

1. Choose a topic and ask a question. Give your reasons, then ask again.

Topic: _____
Question: May I _____
Reasons: 1. (answers will vary)
2. _____
3. _____
4. _____
Ask again: _____

2. Use these sentences to write a paragraph. Write the main idea, add the details, then retell the main idea. Indent the first sentence. Use capitals and periods. Remember to give the paragraph a title.

Paragraphs will vary.

Page 18 — Skill: Compare and Contrast

Some things can be both alike and different.

1. Complete the circles by comparing and contrasting a window and a door.

window contrast	compare	door contrast
1. made of glass	1. opens	1. made of wood
2. smooth	2. in a wall	2. has a knob or handle
3. breaks easily	3. part of a building	3. swings on hinges

2. Write 2 paragraphs below. In the first paragraph tell how windows and doors are alike. Tell how each is different in the second paragraph. Indent the first sentence. Title your story.

Windows and Doors

Windows and doors are a lot alike. They both open and close. They are both part of a building. You find them both in a wall. You can see out of both. Windows and doors let in light and air.

Windows and doors are also different. Windows are made of glass, and can break easily. They are very smooth. Doors are made of wood. They swing on hinges. Doors have a knob in the middle.

Page 19 — Skill: Compare and Contrast

Some things can be both alike and different.

1. Complete the circles by comparing and contrasting an orange and a lemon.

orange contrast	compare	lemon contrast
1. orange	1. juicy	1. yellow
2. round	2. has a peel	2. oval
3. sweet	3. has seeds	3. sour

1. Write 2 paragraphs below. In the first paragraph tell how oranges and lemons are alike. Tell how each is different in the second paragraph. Indent the first sentence. Title your story.

Paragraphs will vary.

Page 20 — Skill: Compare and Contrast

Some things can be both alike and different.

1. Complete the circles by comparing and contrasting a letter and a telephone.

letter contrast	compare	telephone contrast
1. write it	1. delivers messages	1. dial it
2. made of paper	2. connects people	2. made of plastic
3. mail it	3. communication	3. rings

(answers will vary)

2. Write 2 paragraphs below. In the first paragraph tell how a letter and a telephone are alike. Tell how each is different in the second paragraph. Indent the first sentence. Title your story.

Paragraphs will vary.

Answer Key

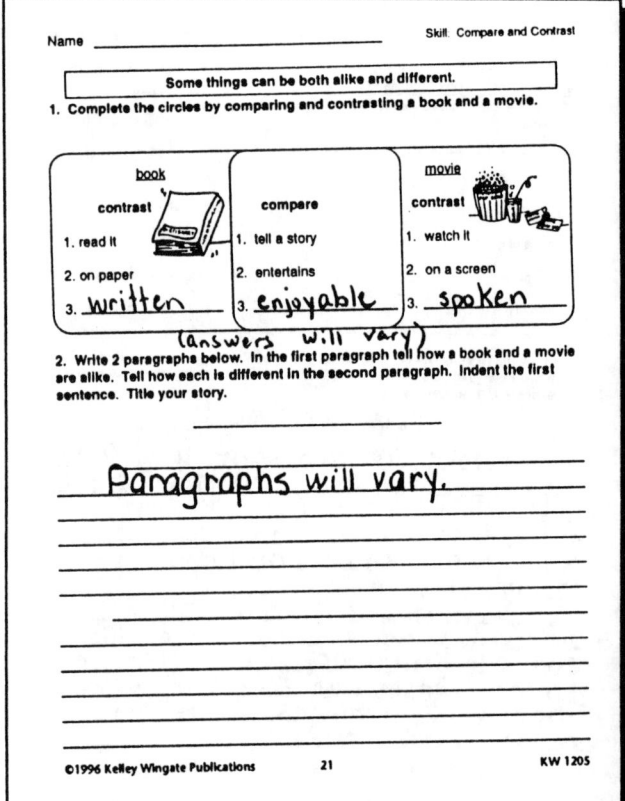

Answer Key

Page 25
Skill: Compare and Contrast

Some things can be both alike and different.

1. Complete the circles by comparing and contrasting a computer and a television.

television — contrast
1. watch it
2. dials
3. change channels

compare
1. screen
2. uses electricity
3. gives info

computer — contrast
1. put in data
2. keyboard
3. work on it

(answers will vary)

2. Write 2 paragraphs below...

Paragraphs will vary.

Page 26
Skill: Compare and Contrast

Some things can be both alike and different.

1. Complete the circles by comparing and contrasting an truck and a car.

truck — contrast
1. bed
2. larger
3. cargo

compare
1. drive it
2. tires
3. vehicles

car — contrast
1. 4 doors
2. smaller
3. passengers

(answers will vary)

2. Write 2 paragraphs below...

Paragraphs will vary.

Page 27
Skill: Compare and Contrast

Some things can be both alike and different.

1. Choose your own topic to compare and contrast.

(answers will vary)

2. Write 2 paragraphs below...

Paragraphs will vary.

Page 28
Skill: Descriptive Writing

Adjectives are words that describe which, how many, what color, or what an object looks or feels like.

1. speedy 2. hot 3. roaring 4. screeching 5. shiny

Hot Rods

This speedy little car is a hot rod. When the flag is dropped it goes roaring down the track. It races against another shiny hot rod for a trophy. At the end of the run both cars come to a screeching halt. Who is the winner?

1. sweet 2. soft 3. picky 4. sharp 5. thorny

Stories will vary.

Answer Key

Name ______________________ Skill: Descriptive Writing

Adjectives are words that describe which, how many, what color, or what an object looks or feels like.

Adjectives make stories more colorful and interesting. They help you "see" a story in your imagination.

Write a paragraph about each picture using the adjectives listed beside it. Write a title for your paragraph.

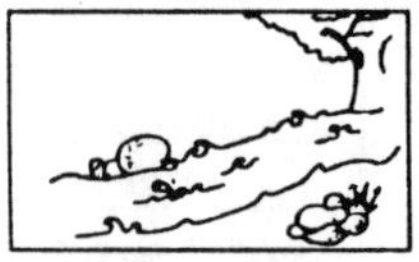

1. splashing 2. rocky
3. icy cold 4. clear
5. gurgling

Stories will vary.

1. juicy 2. greasy
3. tasty 4. mouth watering
5. melted cheese

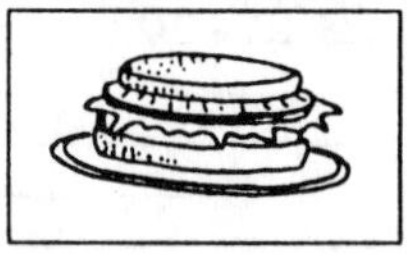

Stories will vary.

©1996 Kelley Wingate Publications 29 KW 1205

Name ______________________ Skill: Descriptive Writing

Adjectives are words that describe which, how many, what color, or what an object looks or feels like.

Adjectives make stories more colorful and interesting. They help you "see" a story in your imagination.

Four adjectives are listed for each picture below. Add an adjective of your own. Write a paragraph about each picture using the adjectives.

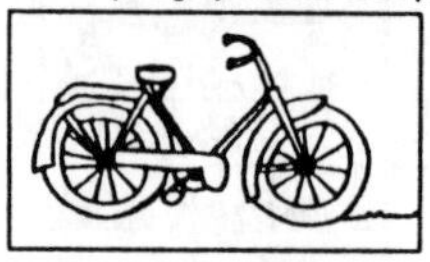

1. fun 2. sparkling
3. new 4. fast
5. shiny (answers will vary)

Stories will vary.

1. red 2. round
3. juicy 4. healthy
5. crisp (answers will vary)

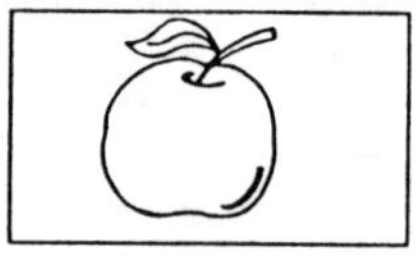

Stories will vary.

©1996 Kelley Wingate Publications 30 KW 1205

Name ______________________ Skill: Descriptive Writing

Adjectives are words that describe which, how many, what color, or what an object looks or feels like.

Adjectives make stories more colorful and interesting. They help you "see" a story in your imagination.

Four adjectives are listed for each picture below. Add an adjective of your own. Write a paragraph about each picture using the adjectives.

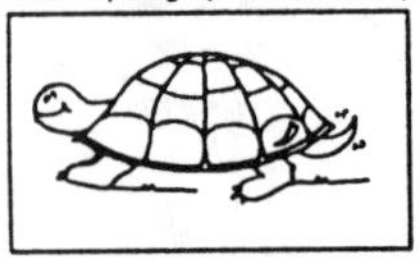

1. green 2. friendly
3. slow 4. hard shelled
5. shy (answers will vary)

Stories will vary.

1. round 2. orange
3. bumpy 4. scary
5. oval (answers will vary)

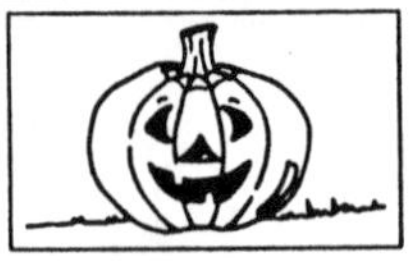

Stories will vary.

©1996 Kelley Wingate Publications 31 KW 1205

Name ______________________ Skill: Descriptive Writing

Adjectives are words that describe which, how many, what color, or what an object looks or feels like.

Adjectives make stories more colorful and interesting. They help you "see" a story in your imagination.

Three adjectives are listed for each picture below. Add two adjectives of your own. Write a paragraph about each picture using the adjectives.

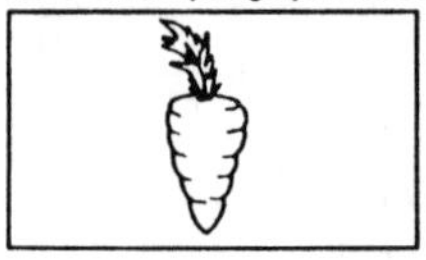

1. orange 2. delicious
3. long 4. crispy
5. crunchy (answers will vary)

Stories will vary.

1. furry 2. long-earred
3. cute 4. soft
5. wiggly (answers will vary)

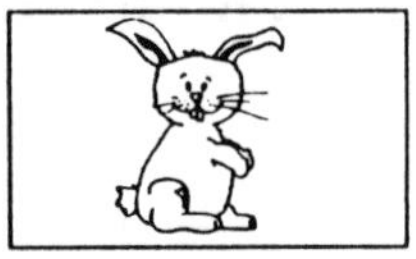

Stories will vary.

©1996 Kelley Wingate Publications 32 KW 1205

Answer Key

Page 33
Three adjectives are listed for each picture below. Add two adjectives of your own. Write a paragraph about each picture using the adjectives.

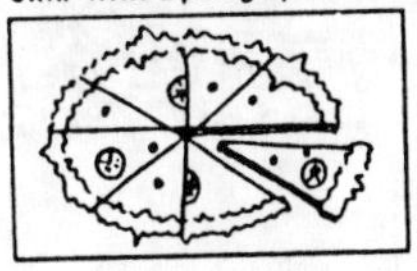

1. hot 2. flavorful 3. round 4. tasty 5. gooey
(answers will vary)

Stories will vary.

1. cold 2. wet 3. sticky 4. yummy 5. smooth
(answers will vary)

Stories will vary.

Page 34
Two adjectives are listed for each picture below. Add three adjectives of your own. Write a paragraph about each picture using the adjectives.

1. green 2. rough skin 3. sharp 4. fierce 5. strong
(answers will vary)

Stories will vary.

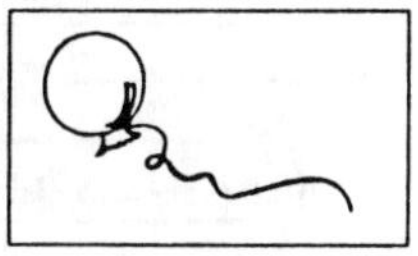

1. fragile 2. light 3. airy 4. smooth 5. fun
(answers will vary)

Stories will vary.

Page 35
Two adjectives are listed for each picture below. Add three adjectives of your own. Write a paragraph about each picture using the adjectives.

1. feathered 2. wise 3. brown 4. eared 5. large
(answers will vary)

Stories will vary.

1. sandy 2. hot 3. dry 4. scorching 5. prickly
(answers will vary)

Stories will vary.

Page 36
For each picture, write five adjectives to describe it. Write a paragraph about each picture using the adjectives. Give each paragraph a title.

1. starched 2. ironed 3. clean 4. fresh 5. crisp
(answers will vary)

Stories will vary.

1. bubbly 2. long 3. colorful 4. quick 5. happy
(answers will vary)

Stories will vary.

Answer Key

Answers will vary throughout (pages 37–40).

Answer Key

Page 41
1. Who or what is this story about? Answers will vary.

Stories will vary.

Page 42
1. Who or what is this story about? Answers will vary.

Stories will vary.

Page 43

Word Box:
- leaves
- sunshine
- breeze
- nap

(answers will vary)

Sally Snail

Sally Snail loves lazy afternoons. She sits in a tree in the warm sunshine. A gentle breeze touches the leaves. Sally slowly stretches her antlers. It is cozy inside her swirling shell. Perhaps she will take a nap.

Page 44

Word Box:
- smoke
- caboose
- fast
- loud

(answers will vary)

Stories will vary.

Answer Key

Worksheet 1 (page 45): Picture of racers at FINISH line.
Word Box: race, fast, tie, racers | hot, fun, running, winner
(answers will vary)
Stories will vary.

Worksheet 2 (page 46): Picture of girl in rain.
Word Box: raincoat, puddles, splash, storm | muddy, wet, fun, boots
(answers will vary)
Stories will vary.

Worksheet 3 (page 47): Picture of castle.
Word Box: moat, knights, King, queen | tower, old, duel, horses
(answers will vary)
Stories will vary.

Worksheet 4 (page 48): Picture of farm.
Word Box: farm, morning, rooster, sunrise | hay, barn, chores, fresh
(answers will vary)
Stories will vary.

Answer Key

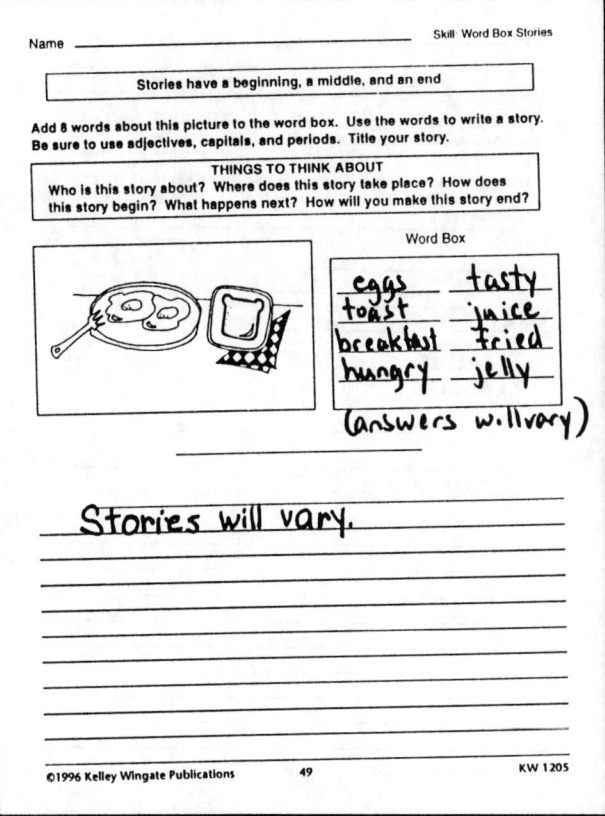

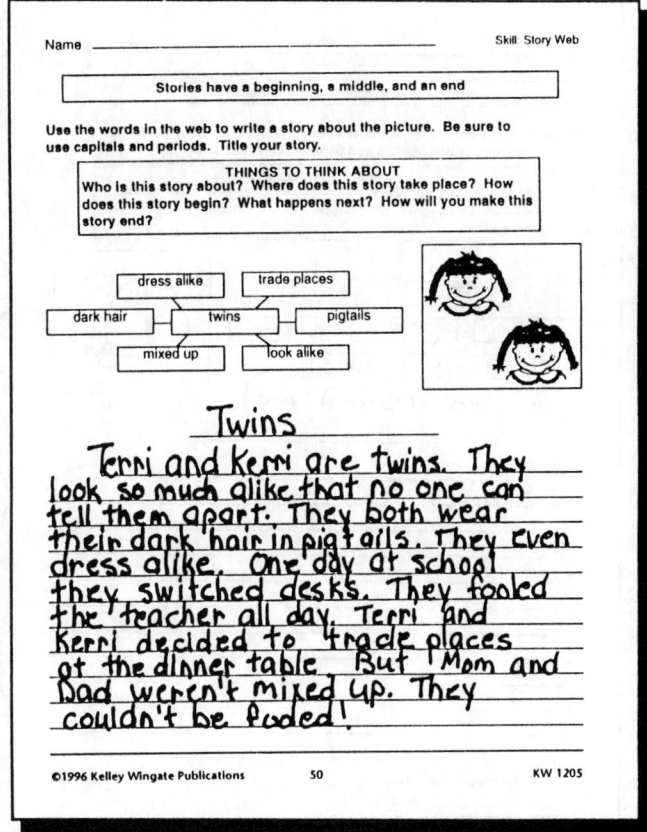

Answer Key

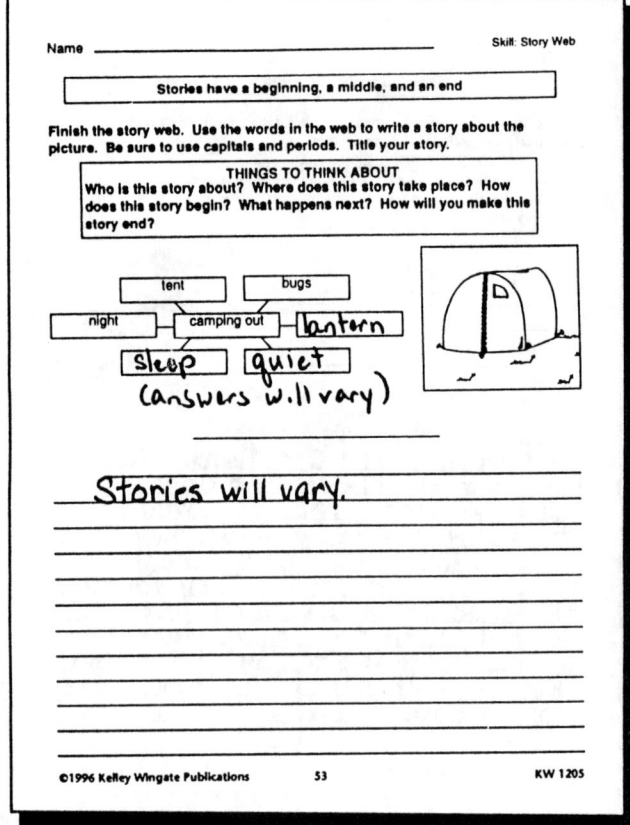
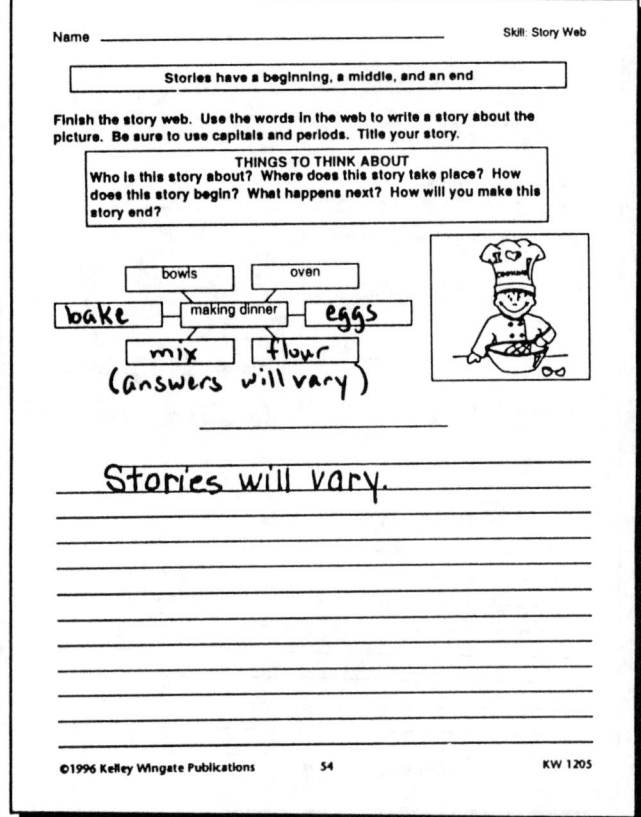

Answer Key

Name ______________________ Skill: Writing Stories

THINGS TO THINK ABOUT FOR EVERY STORY:

- ★ Sentences begin with capitals and end with periods, question marks, or exclamation marks.
- ★ A paragraph contains a main idea and supporting details.
- ★ The first sentence of a paragraph should be indented.
- ★ Adjectives make stories more colorful and interesting.
- ★ A story tells who did what, when and where it was done, how it happened, and why it happened.
- ★ Stories have a beginning, a middle, and an end.

Write a story about the picture below. Be sure to follow all the hints in the "Things to Think About" box. Give your story a title.

Stories will vary.

©1996 Kelley Wingate Publications 57 KW 1205

Name ______________________ Skill: Writing Stories

THINGS TO THINK ABOUT FOR EVERY STORY:

- ★ Sentences begin with capitals and end with periods, question marks, or exclamation marks.
- ★ A paragraph contains a main idea and supporting details.
- ★ The first sentence of a paragraph should be indented.
- ★ Adjectives make stories more colorful and interesting.
- ★ A story tells who did what, when and where it was done, how it happened, and why it happened.
- ★ Stories have a beginning, a middle, and an end.

Write a story about the picture below. Be sure to follow all the hints in the "Things to Think About" box. Give your story a title.

Stories will vary.

©1996 Kelley Wingate Publications 58 KW 1205

Name ______________________ Skill: Writing Stories

THINGS TO THINK ABOUT FOR EVERY STORY:

- ★ Sentences begin with capitals and end with periods, question marks, or exclamation marks.
- ★ A paragraph contains a main idea and supporting details.
- ★ The first sentence of a paragraph should be indented.
- ★ Adjectives make stories more colorful and interesting.
- ★ A story tells who did what, when and where it was done, how it happened, and why it happened.
- ★ Stories have a beginning, a middle, and an end.

Write a story about the picture below. Be sure to follow all the hints in the "Things to Think About" box. Give your story a title.

Stories will vary.

©1996 Kelley Wingate Publications 59 KW 1205

Name ______________________ Skill: Writing Stories

THINGS TO THINK ABOUT FOR EVERY STORY:

- ★ Sentences begin with capitals and end with periods, question marks, or exclamation marks.
- ★ A paragraph contains a main idea and supporting details.
- ★ The first sentence of a paragraph should be indented.
- ★ Adjectives make stories more colorful and interesting.
- ★ A story tells who did what, when and where it was done, how it happened, and why it happened.
- ★ Stories have a beginning, a middle, and an end.

Write a story about the picture below. Be sure to follow all the hints in the "Things to Think About" box. Give your story a title.

Stories will vary.

©1996 Kelley Wingate Publications 60 KW 1205

Answer Key

Stories will vary. (pages 61, 62, 63, 64)

Answer Key

Page 65 — Skill: Writing Stories

THINGS TO THINK ABOUT FOR EVERY STORY:
- Sentences begin with capitals and end with periods, question marks, or exclamation marks.
- A paragraph contains a main idea and supporting details.
- The first sentence of a paragraph should be indented.
- Adjectives make stories more colorful and interesting.
- A story tells who did what, when and where it was done, how it happened, and why it happened.
- Stories have a beginning, a middle, and an end.

Write a story about the picture below. Be sure to follow all the hints in the "Things to Think About" box. Give your story a title.

Stories will vary.

Page 66 — Skill: Three Paragraph Stories

Putting Paragraphs Together
- Each paragraph in a story contains a main idea and supporting details.
- The opening paragraph gives the topic of the story. It should catch the interest of the reader.
- The second paragraph gives more information about the topic of the story.
- The last paragraph reviews the main idea and ends the story.

Use the information contained in this outline to write a three paragraph story. Use an extra sheet of paper if you need more space.

Title: The School Fair
Main Idea: I. Games to play
Details:
  A. relay races
  B. ring toss
  C. basketball throw
Main Idea: II. Food to eat
  A. pizza
  B. popcorn
  C. candy
Main Idea: III. Love the fair
  A. face painted
  B. win prizes
  C. run with friends

The School Fair

It's time for the school fair! There will be relay races, a ring toss, and a basketball throw.

I can't wait to taste the pizza, popcorn, and cotton candy.

I love the school fair. I'll get my face painted, win lots of prizes, and have a good time with all my friends.

Page 67 — Skill: Three Paragraph Stories

Putting Paragraphs Together
- Each paragraph in a story contains a main idea and supporting details.
- The opening paragraph gives the topic of the story. It should catch the interest of the reader.
- The second paragraph gives more information about the topic of the story.
- The last paragraph reviews the main idea and ends the story.

Use the information contained in this outline to write a three paragraph story. Use an extra sheet of paper if you need more space.

Title: Camping
Main Idea: I. Get camping gear
Details:
  A. check tent
  B. test flashlights
  C. pack food
Main Idea: II. Set up camp
  A. find a spot
  B. pitch tent
  C. build campfire pit
Main Idea: III. Enjoy the trip
  A. take hikes
  B. go fishing
  C. cook over the fire

Stories will vary.

Page 68 — Skill: Three Paragraph Stories

Putting Paragraphs Together
- Each paragraph in a story contains a main idea and supporting details.
- The opening paragraph gives the topic of the story. It should catch the interest of the reader.
- The second paragraph gives more information about the topic of the story.
- The last paragraph reviews the main idea and ends the story.

Add your own details then use the information contained in this outline to write a three paragraph story. Use an extra sheet of paper if you need more space.

Title: Rub-A-Dub Dog
Main Idea: I. Getting ready
Details:
  A. fill tub with water
  B. get shampoo and towels
  C. get in
Main Idea: II. Bath time
  A. squirt the shampoo
  B. lather the dog
  C. wash the dog
Main Idea: III. Clean and happy
  A. dry the dog with towels
  B. brush the fur
  C. hug the dog

(details will vary)

Stories will vary.

Answer Key

Page 69 — Painting the Porch
- I. Porch needed painting
  - A. paint was peeling
  - B. looked shabby
  - C. needed paint
- II. Worked all weekend
  - A. scraped off old paint
  - B. washed down the walls
  - C. painted
- III. Looks like new
  - A. fresh bright paint
  - B. looks clean and nice
  - C. good job

(details will vary)

Stories will vary.

Page 70 — Visit to the Dentist
- I. Painful tooth
  - A. bit into a candied apple
  - B. stuck to teeth
  - C. lost my tooth
- II. Called the dentist
  - A. told nurse the problem
  - B. got appointment
  - C. went in
- III. Saw the dentist
  - A. took x-rays of my tooth
  - B. cleaned my teeth
  - C. gave me toothbrush

(details will vary)

Stories will vary.

Page 71 — The Science Project Contest
- I. Decide on a project
  - A. plan the topic
  - B. design project
  - C. begin research
- II. Find out the facts
  - A. look in books
  - B. use computer
  - C. write report
- III. Make the project
  - A. get materials
  - B. make project
  - C. label parts

(details will vary)

Stories will vary.

Page 72
(Title, main ideas, and details will vary)

Stories will vary.

Answer Key

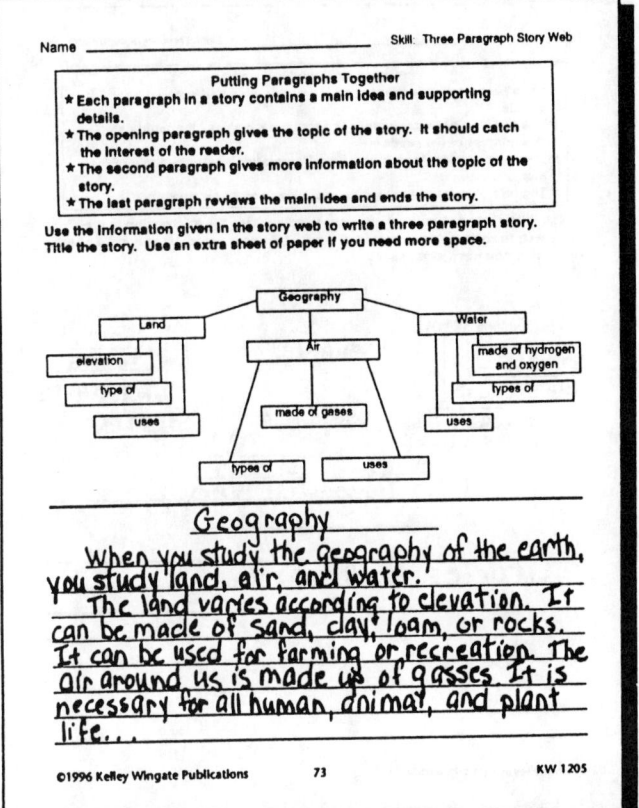

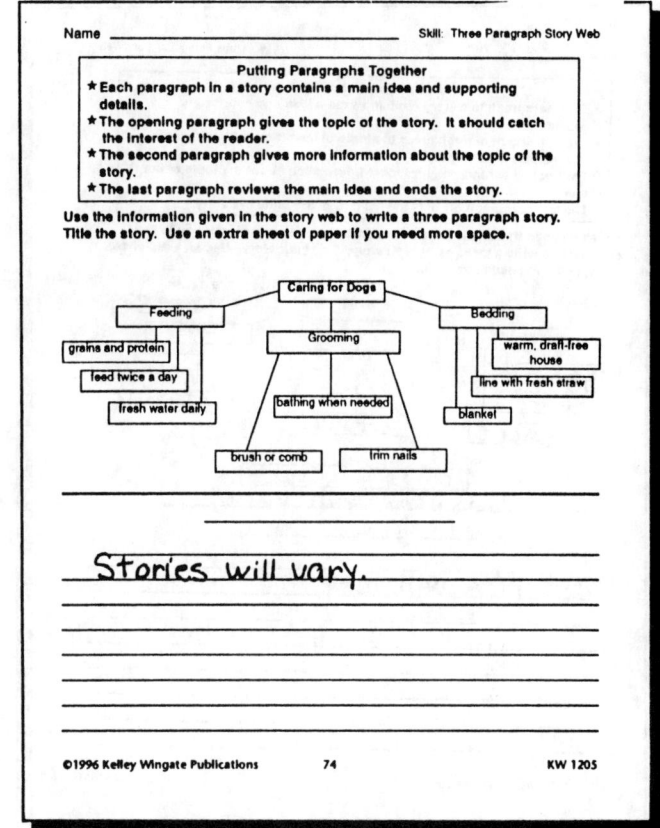

125 CD-3720

Answer Key

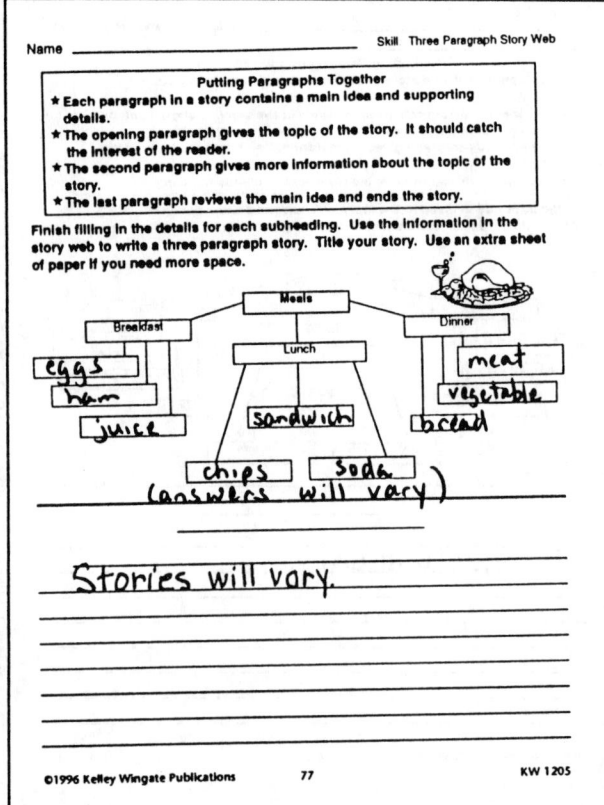

Answer Key

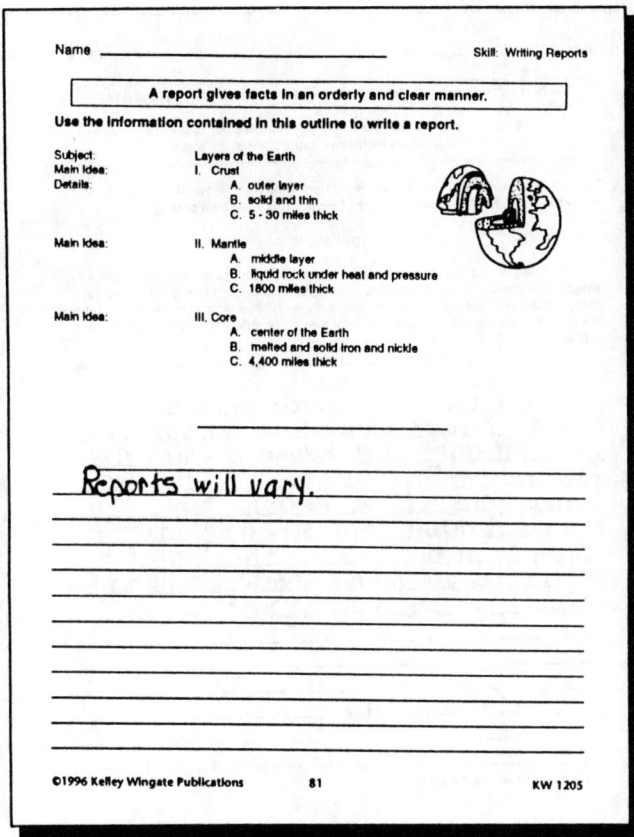

Answer Key

Page 85 — Skill: Writing Reports

A report gives facts in an orderly and clear manner.

Choose a topic and write the information in this outline. Use the information to write a report.

Subject:
Main Idea: I.
Details: A.
                     B.
                     C.

Main Idea: II.
                    A.
                    B.
                    C.

Main Idea: III.
                     A.
                     B.
                     C.

(Subjects, main idea, and details will vary)

Reports will vary.

Page 86 — Skill: Point of View

The **first person** point of view tells a story as if the narrator were a part of it. This view uses the words "I", "me", or "we".
The **third person** point of view tells the story as if the narrator were watching it happen. This view uses the words "he", "she", "they", or "them".

This story is written from the first person point of view. Rewrite the story, changing it to the third person point of view. Add your own ending.

The Rescue

My friends and I were at the beach. We were laying in the sun and watching the seagulls overhead. It was a beautiful, relaxing day. I thought I heard a faint cry for help. I listened closely and looked around the beach. I heard it again, but saw nothing unusual on the beach. I looked out at the water and spotted a head bobbing in the waves. I....

The Rescue

She and her friends were at the beach. It was a beautiful relaxing day. She thought she heard a faint cry for help. She listened closely and looked around the beach. She heard it again, but saw nothing unusual on the beach. She looked out at the water and spotted a head bobbing in the waves. She ...

Endings will vary.

Page 87 — Skill: Point of View

The **first person** point of view tells a story as if the narrator were a part of it. This view uses the words "I", "me", or "we".
The **third person** point of view tells the story as if the narrator were watching it happen. This view uses the words "he", "she", "they", or "them".

This story is written from the first person point of view. Rewrite the story, changing it to the third person point of view. Add your own ending.

Hang on for Dear Life

I had never ridden a horse before, and I was not sure I wanted to now. My friend, Susie, was sure I would love it. I climbed in the saddle and took the reins in my hands. Susie was beside me on her horse. We started off slowly. I began to relax and almost enjoyed myself. The rocking of the saddle was rather pleasant after all. Just then a rabbit darted out in front of us. My horse....

Endings will vary.

Page 88 — Skill: Point of View

The **first person** point of view tells a story as if the narrator were a part of it. This view uses the words "I", "me", or "we".
The **third person** point of view tells the story as if the narrator were watching it happen. This view uses the words "he", "she", "they", or "them".

This story is written from the first person point of view. Rewrite the story, changing it to the third person point of view. Add your own ending.

Gotcha!

I plopped down on my bed and took off my slippers. It had been a very long day and I was totally worn out. I yawned tiredly and pulled back the covers. That pillow looked so inviting! I could hardly keep my eyes open any more. I sat on the edge of the bed and reached over to turn off the lamp. Just as the light went out I felt something grab my ankle! It pulled me....

Endings will vary.

Answer Key

(Worksheets 89, 90, 91: "Endings will vary.")

Worksheet 92 — Character Webs, Goldilocks and the Three Bears:

Goldilocks was not a polite young lady. She went into the three bears' house when no one was home. Goldilocks didn't respect the bears' property. She ate their food without being invited. She slept in the Baby Bear's bed. She was trespassing! What a selfish girl Goldilocks was.

Answer Key

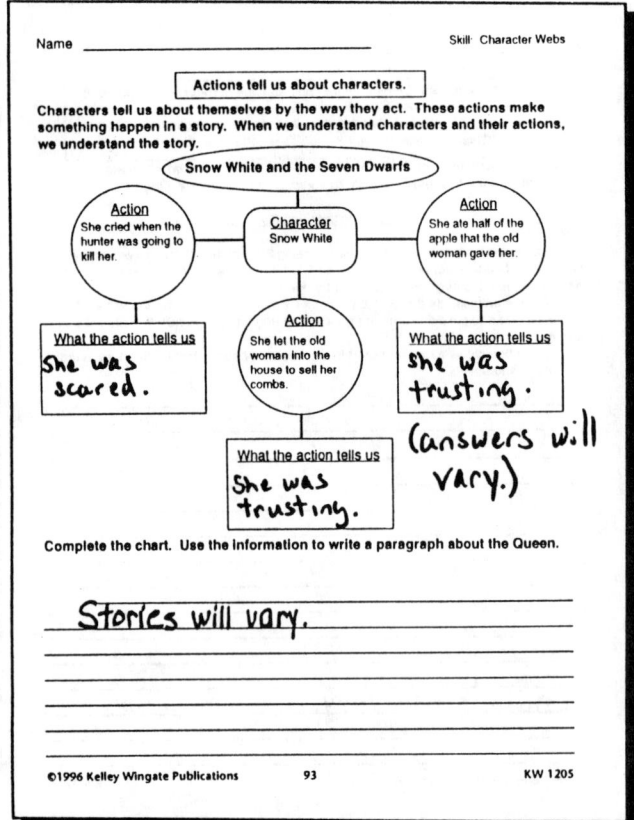

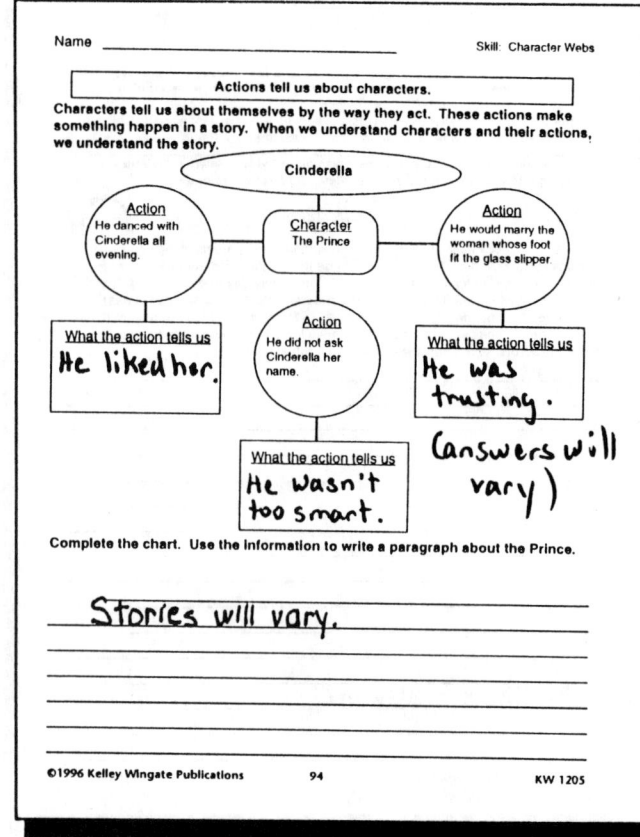

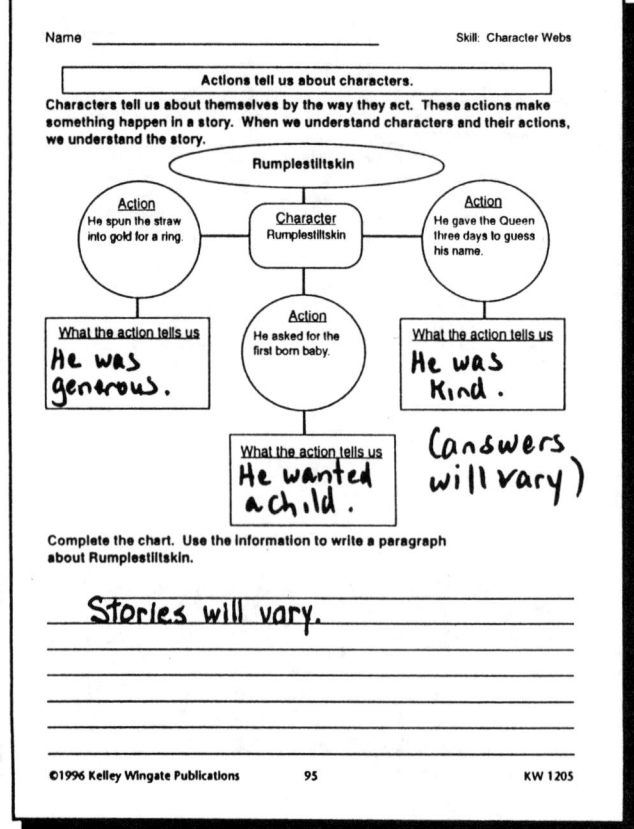

alien	apartment	balance	bluster
Chinese	closing	collect	commercial
compare	connect	contest	contrast
cruise	daily	deliver	dentist

depend	deserted	diet	drench
elevation	energy	entertain	express
freight	friendly	frosty	gear
geography	glider	grain	greasy

greeting	groom	guitar	hurricane
husky	hydrogen	information	insect
instrument	invite	locomotive	mantle
marshmallow	melted	message	mobile

muscle	narrator	nervous	oxygen
pagoda	painful	paragraph	pillow
porch	pressure	prize	product
project	protein	range	rein

relax	relay	rumpled	satellite
scrape	screech	shabby	shampoo
signature	slick	smooth	sparkle
speedy	stadium	strum	tasty

tense	topic	vegetable	yield
temple	timid	twin	wrinkle
temperature	tide	towel	webbed
telephone	thorny	tornado	warn